INSPIRATION BOUQUETS

IN MANY FORMS

A bride shines all the more if she has a beautiful bouquet in her hand. The shape of the bouquet and the types of flowers mostly depend on the bride's personality and the style of the wedding. From stately traditional to informal chic, there is just the right bouquet for every bride. The florist applies the bride's wishes in his/her creation while adding a personal and unique touch to the festivities. Paging through 'In Love: Inspirational European Wedding Bouquets' you will find more than 60 ideas.

Current trends lean towards romantic wild bouquets. A wedding bouquet that looks like you picked the flowers directly from nature straight from the garden. A nonchalant, but structured wealth of florals that comes together in a bouquet. Especially summer flowers make such a bouquet a great idea.

But compact, powerful bouquets remain the most popular. Roses in all their shapes and colors are ideal. You can also choose a structured bouquet and a specific shape which the bride will adore: square, circle, cascade... In this release you will even find several bouquets inspired by perfume bottles. A wedding bouquet in the form of her favorite perfume, isn't that a great idea?

If we look at the types of flowers that are used in bridal bouquets, we often see roses, orchids, calla's ... but florists can also make beautiful bouquets using less popular flowers like chrysanthemums or sunflowers. Perhaps the bride has a favorite flower that can be used in the bouquet. It is also always a good idea to take the season in mind. Is the wedding in summer? Then it would be a shame to use tulips.

Some souvenirs are of great value to the couple and they would like to be very close to them on that special day. In a number of bouquets, you will find old jewels, pearls, pieces of fabric... beautifully arranged among the flowers.

'In Love: Inspirational European Wedding Bouquets' gives you inspiration for bouquets of many different forms: from romantic fine to bold and even cool bouquets. Hand-tied, with floral foam, pouch or drip-shaped. Cherished by every bride.

LOVELY ROMANTIC

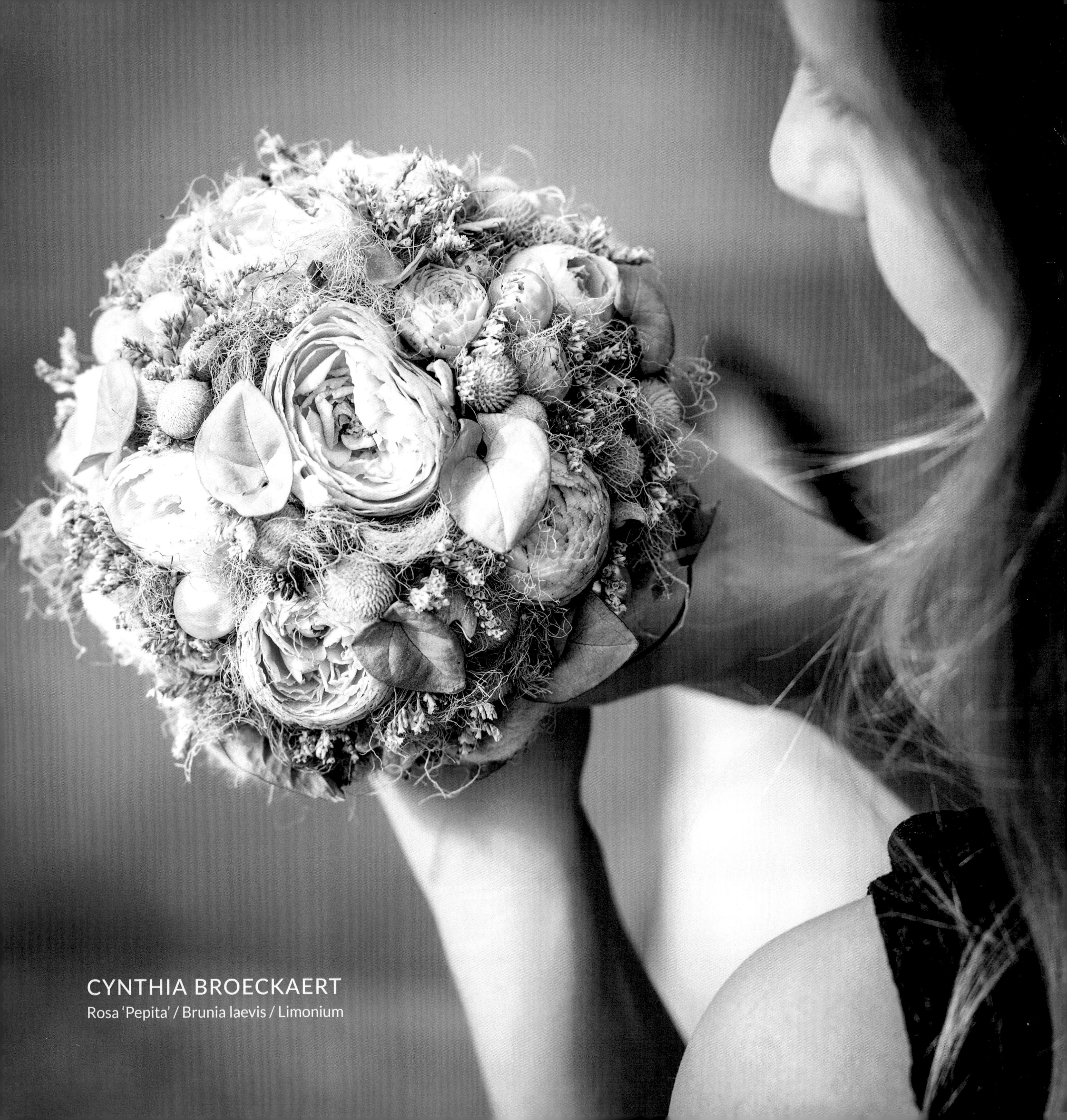

CYNTHIA BROECKAERT

Rosa 'Pepita' / Brunia laevis / Limonium

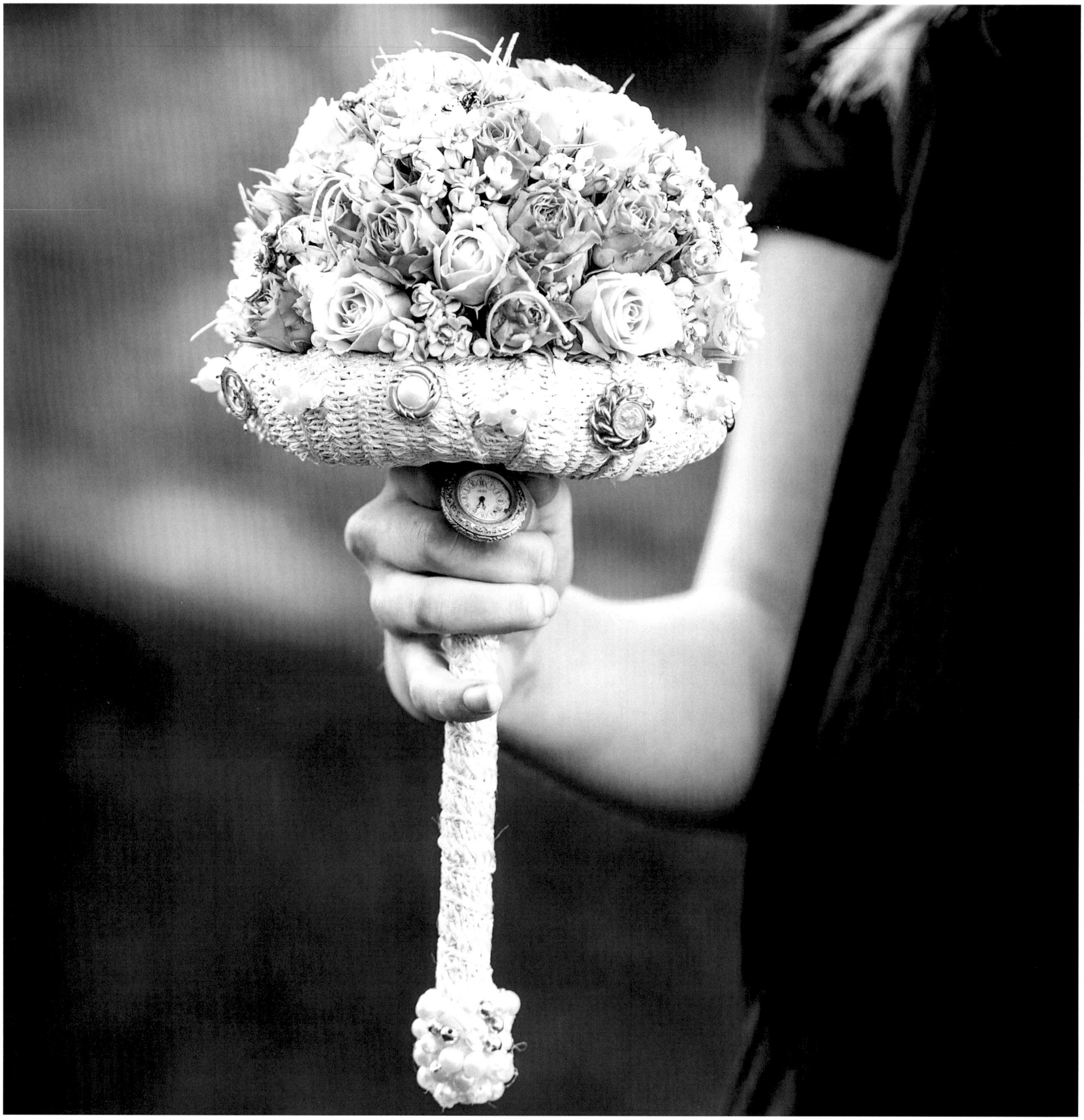

KATHLEEN HENDRIKX

Rosa 'Apricot Nectar' / Bouvardia 'Diamond Lightpink' / Tillandsia cyanea / Rosa 'Metallic Sensation'

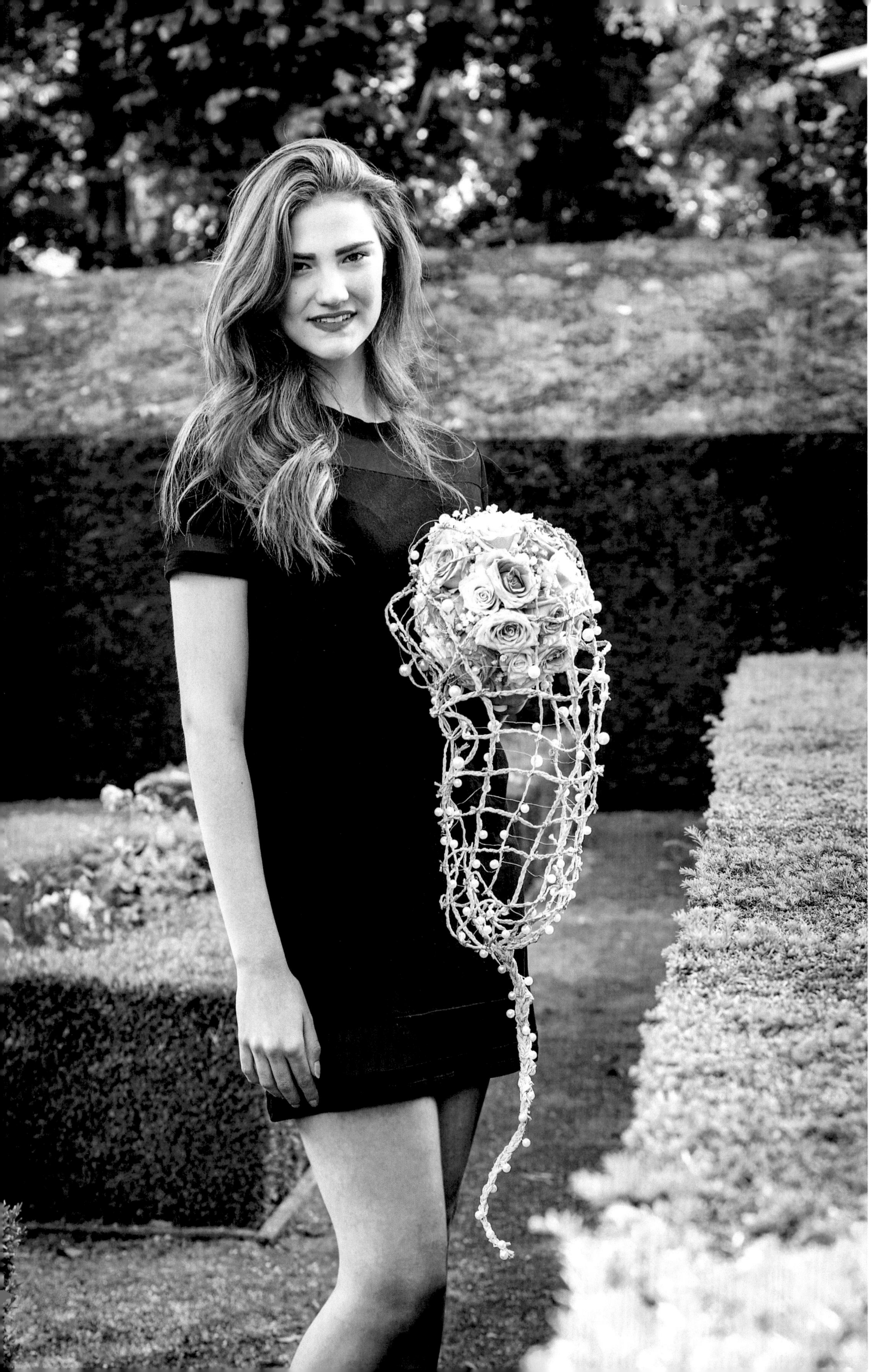

YVON VERMEERE
Rosa / Gypsophilla

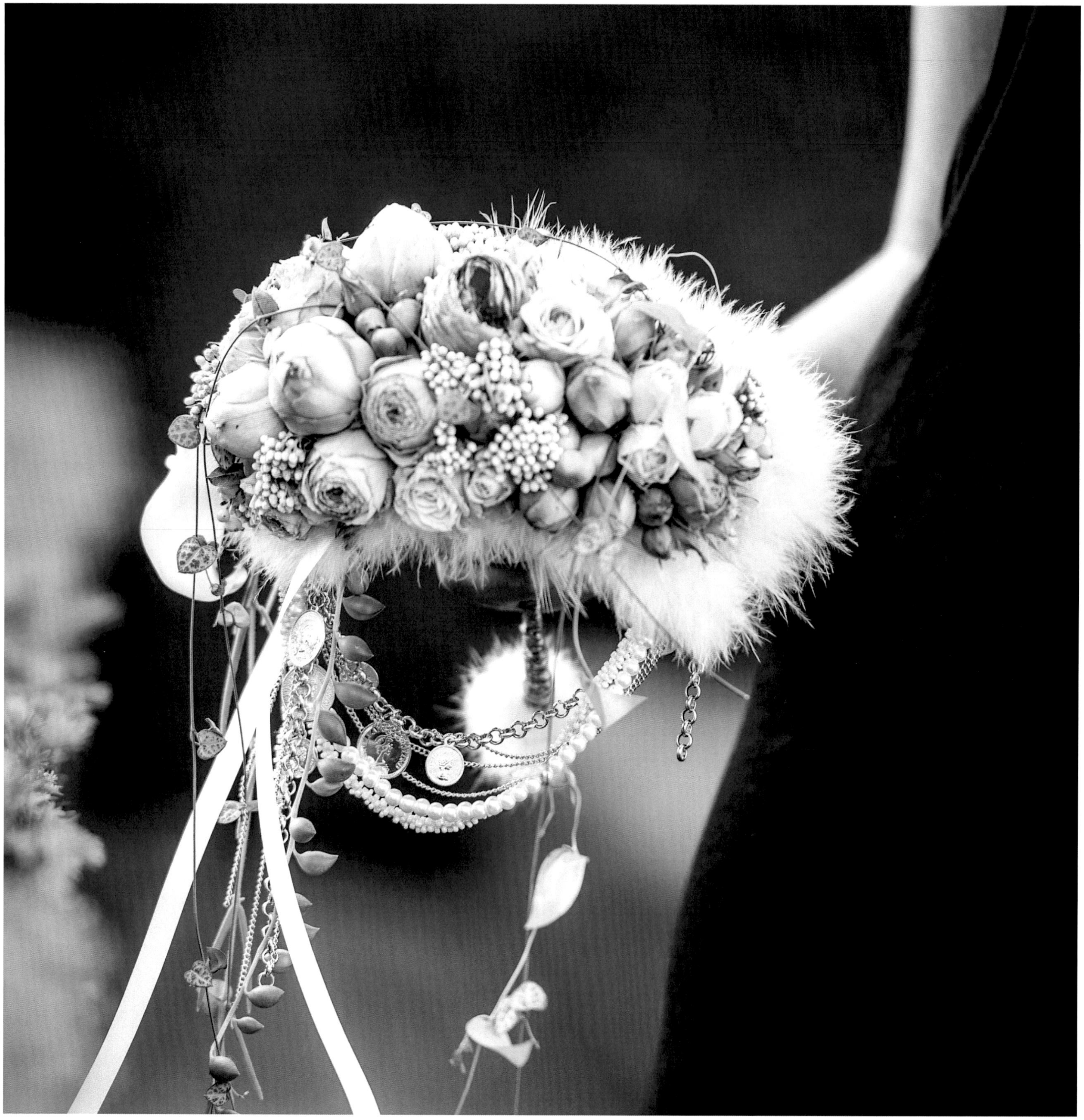

ILSE PALMAERS
Rosa / Ozothamnus / Symphoricarpos / Ceropegia woodii / Senecia rowleyanus

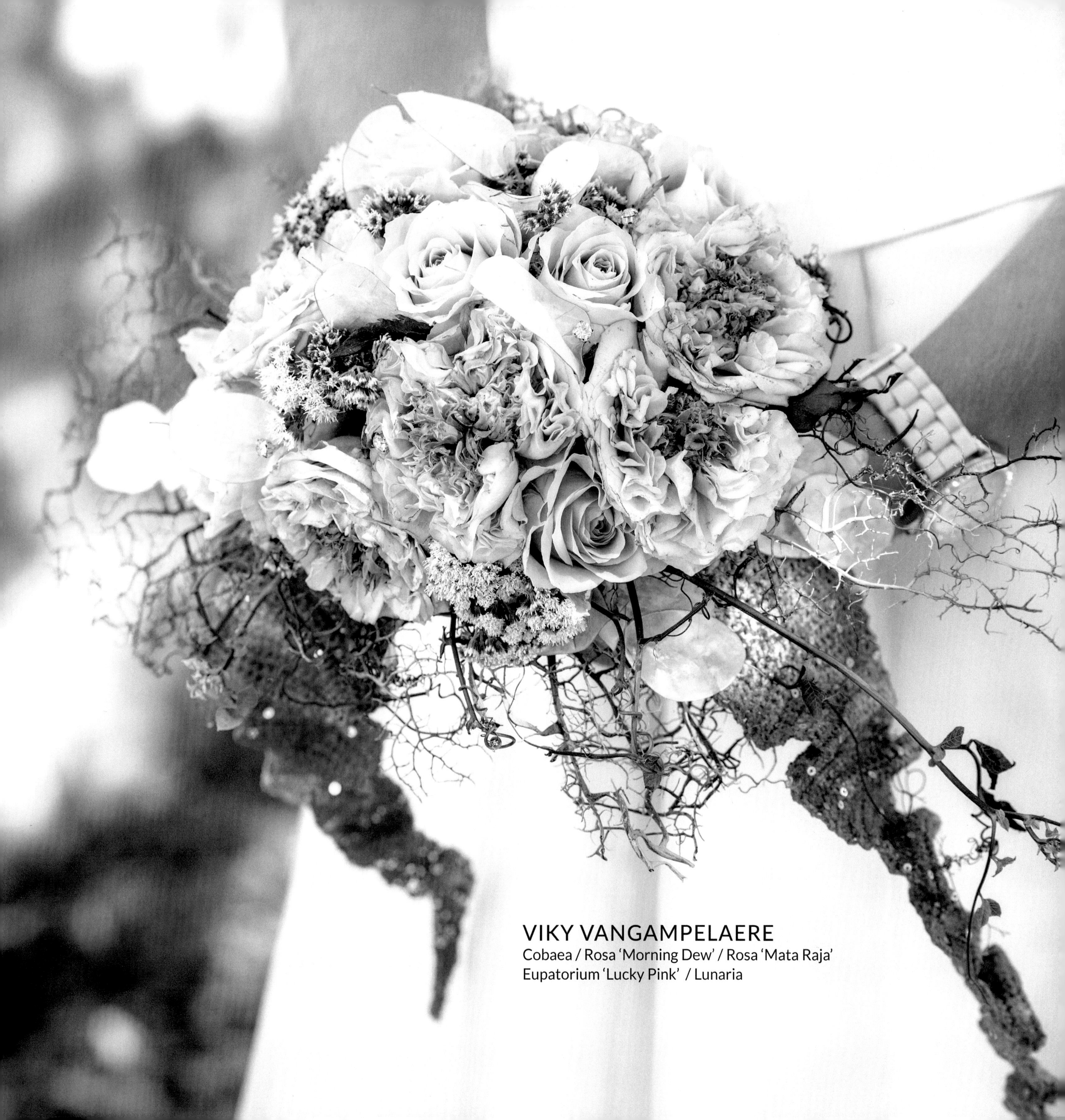

VIKY VANGAMPELAERE
Cobaea / Rosa 'Morning Dew' / Rosa 'Mata Raja'
Eupatorium 'Lucky Pink' / Lunaria

MARTINE
MEEUWSSEN
Phalaenopsis / Craspedia

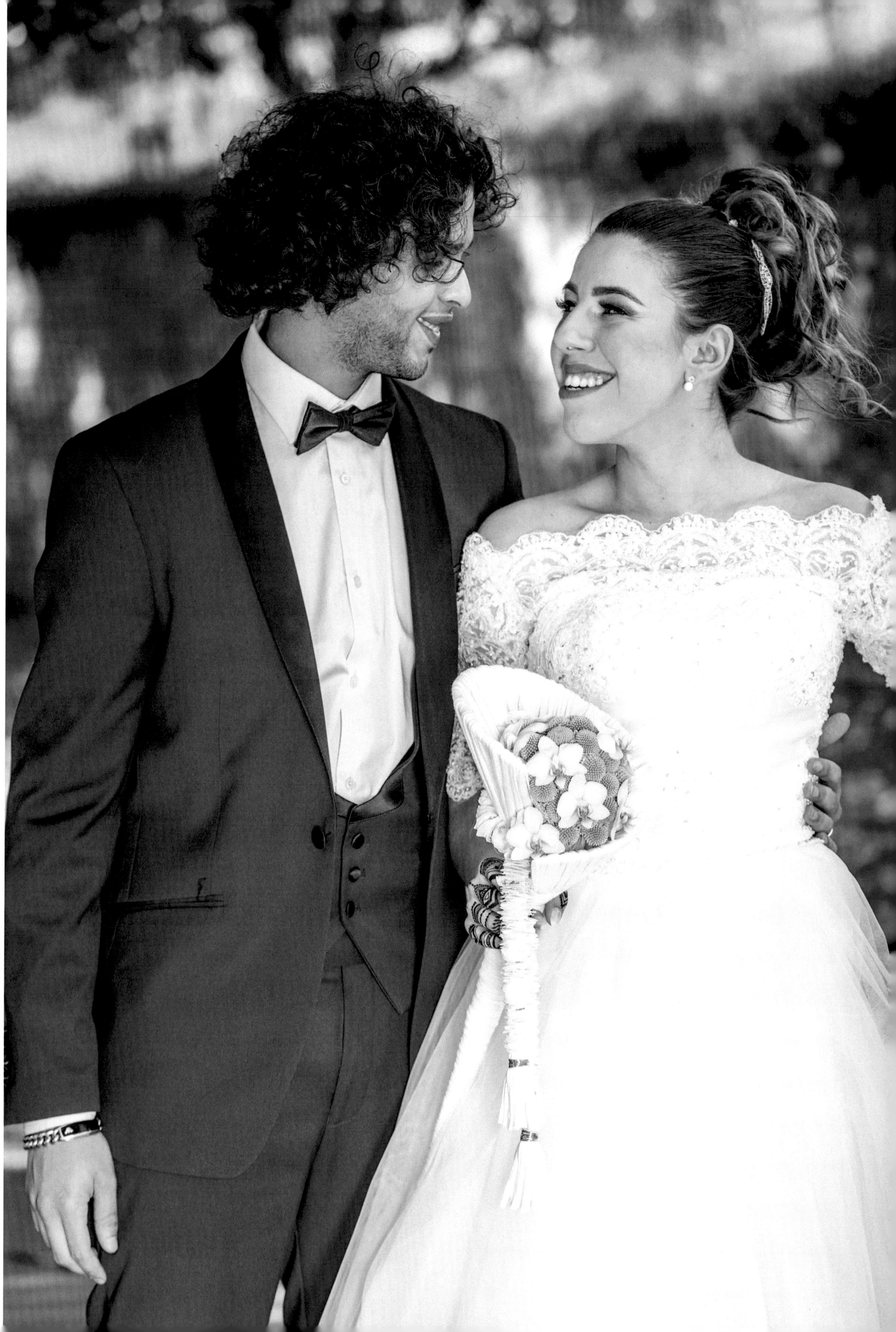

"LOVE IS IN THE AIR"

CÉLINE MOUREAU

Phoenix dactylifera
Chamelaucium
Stachys byzantina
Cortaderia selloana

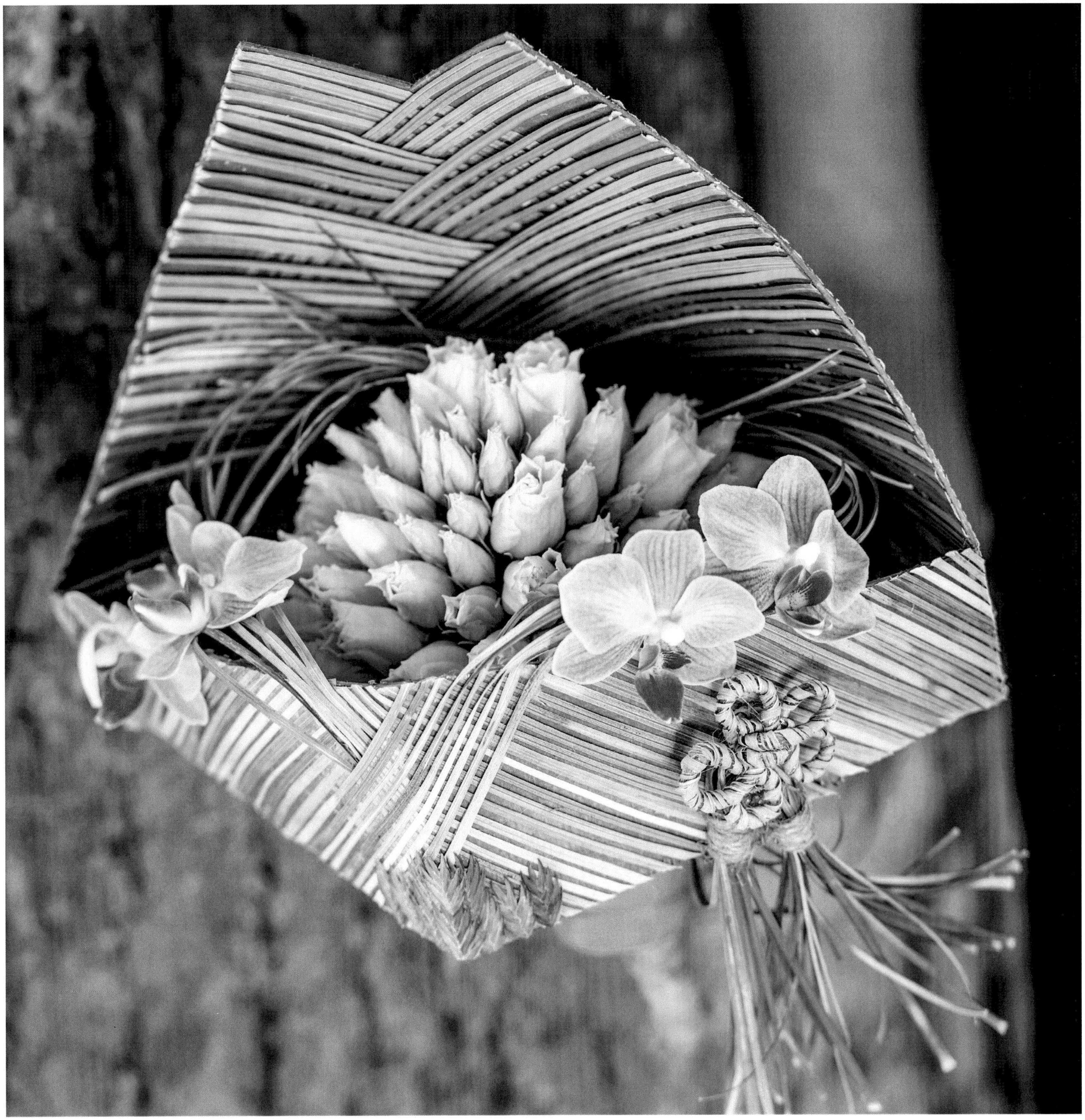

MIEKE HOFLACK

Xerophyllum tenax / Lisianthus / Phalaenopsis / Briza

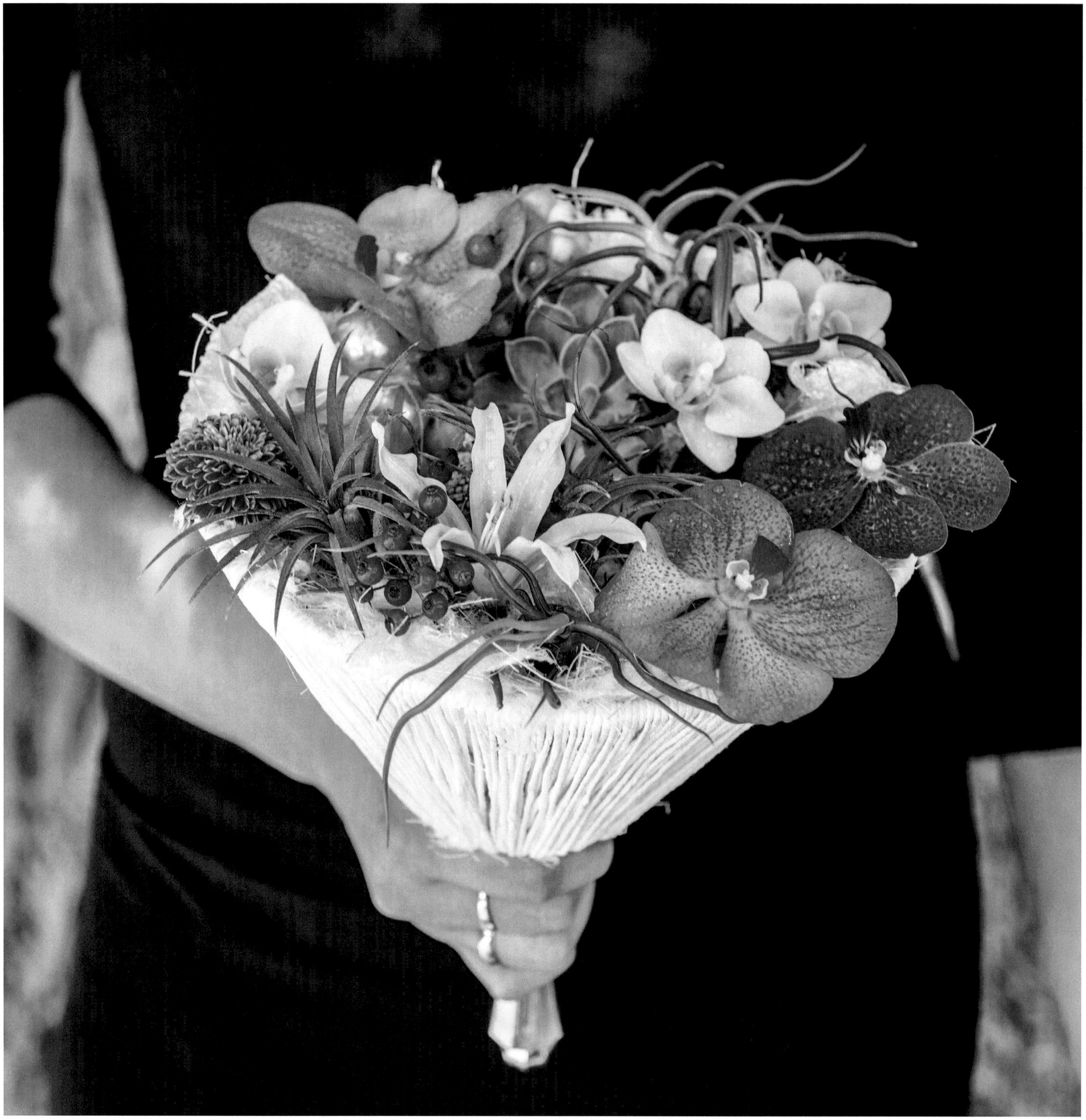

PIRJO KOPPI

Vanda coerulea / Phalaenopsis hybr. / Rosa, Rose hips / Chrysanthemun Santini / Echeveria / Craspedia globosa / Gloriosa 'Rotschildiana' / Symphoricarpos albus / Asclepias tuberosa

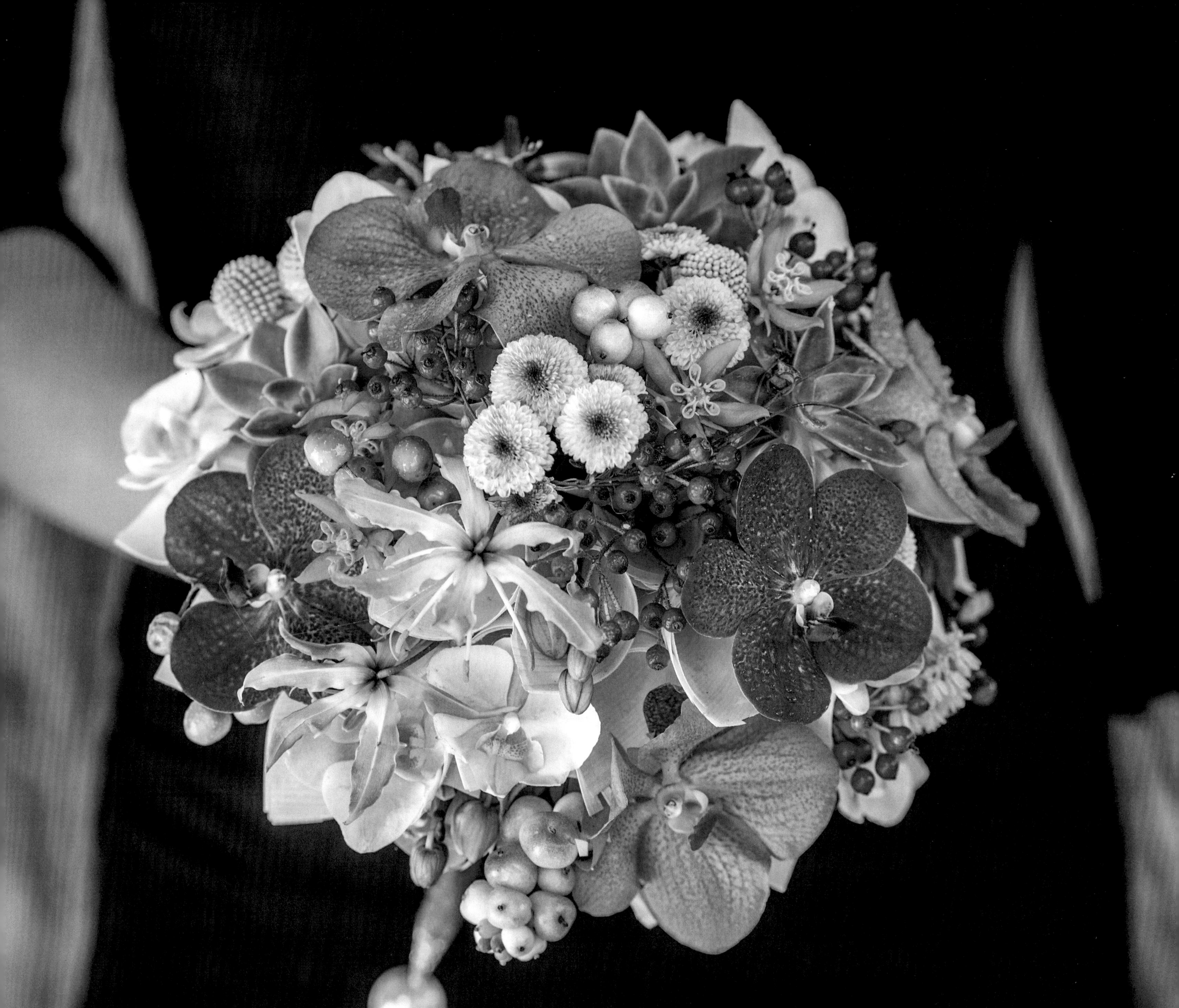

PIRJO KOPPI

Vanda coerulea / Phalaenopsis / Rosa, Rose hips / Chrysanthemun Santini / Echeveria / Craspedia globosa / Gloriosa 'Rotschildiana' / Symphoricarpos albus / Asclepias tuberosa

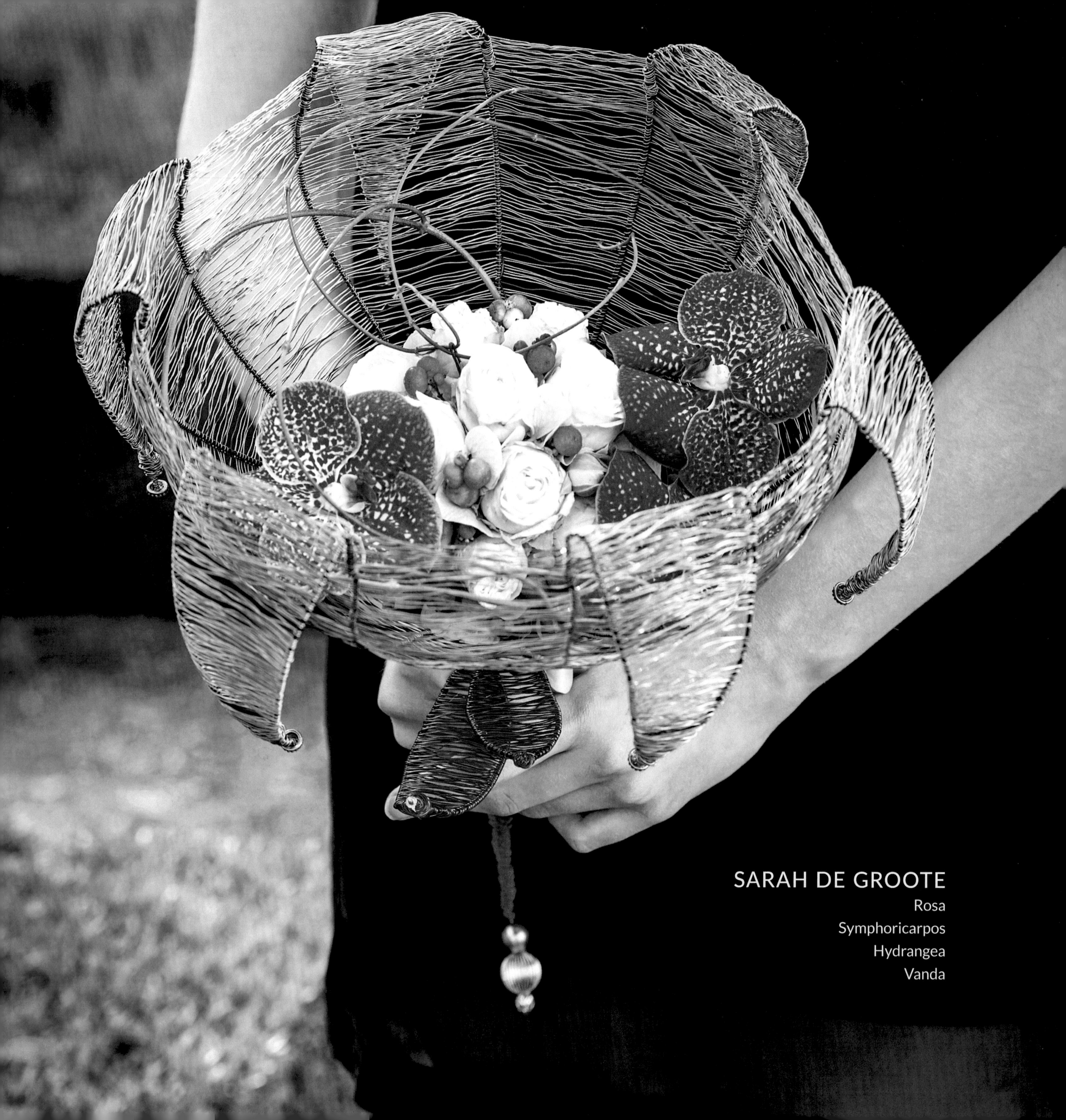

SARAH DE GROOTE
Rosa
Symphoricarpos
Hydrangea
Vanda

"LOVE SEES ROSES WITHOUT THORNS"

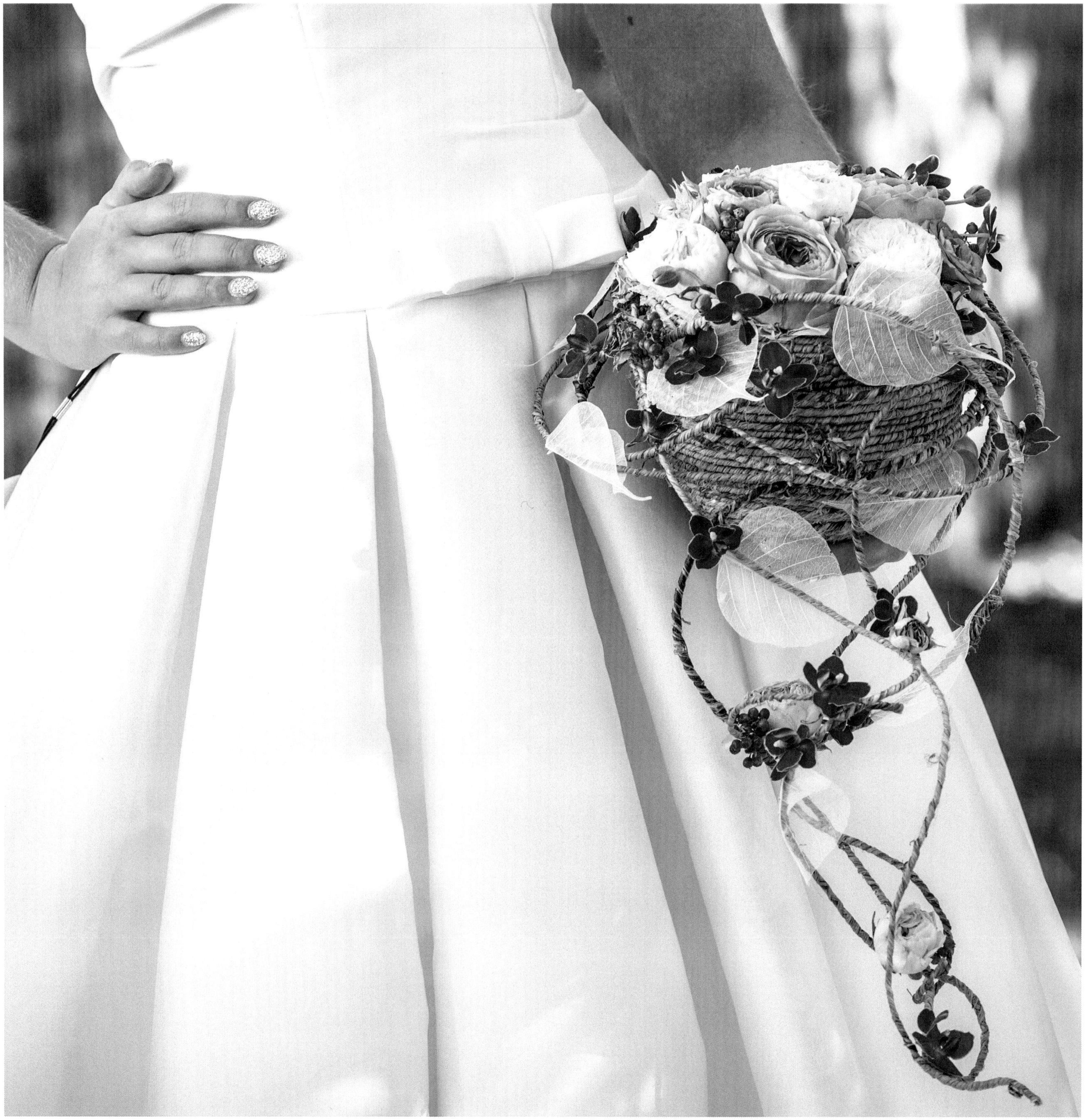

ROY HUTJENS

Rosa / Phalaenopsis mini / Schinus terebinthifolius

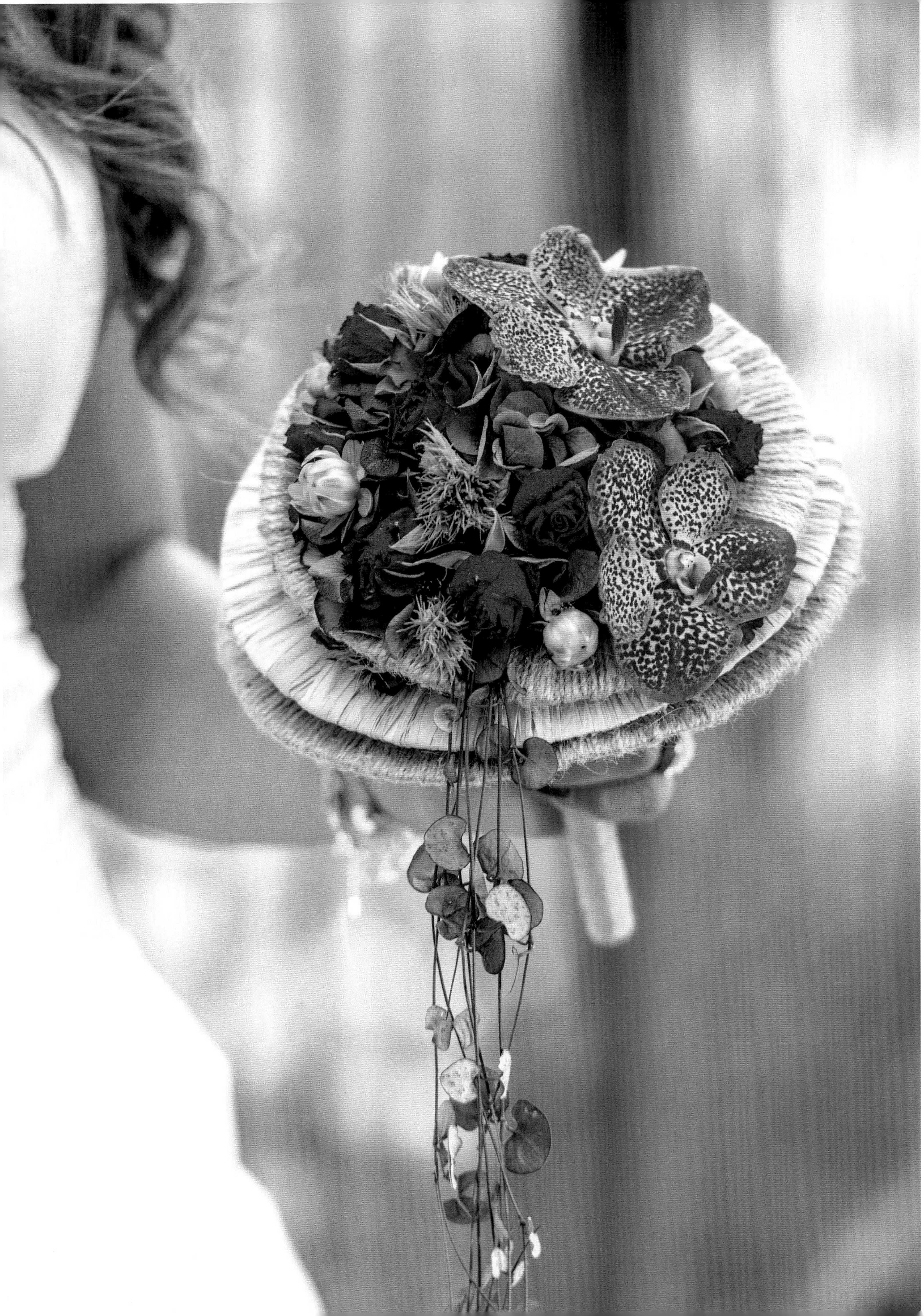

FLORENCE SERVAIS

Rosa
Hydrangea
Dahlia
Dianthus 'Green Trick'
Ceropegia woodii
Vanda

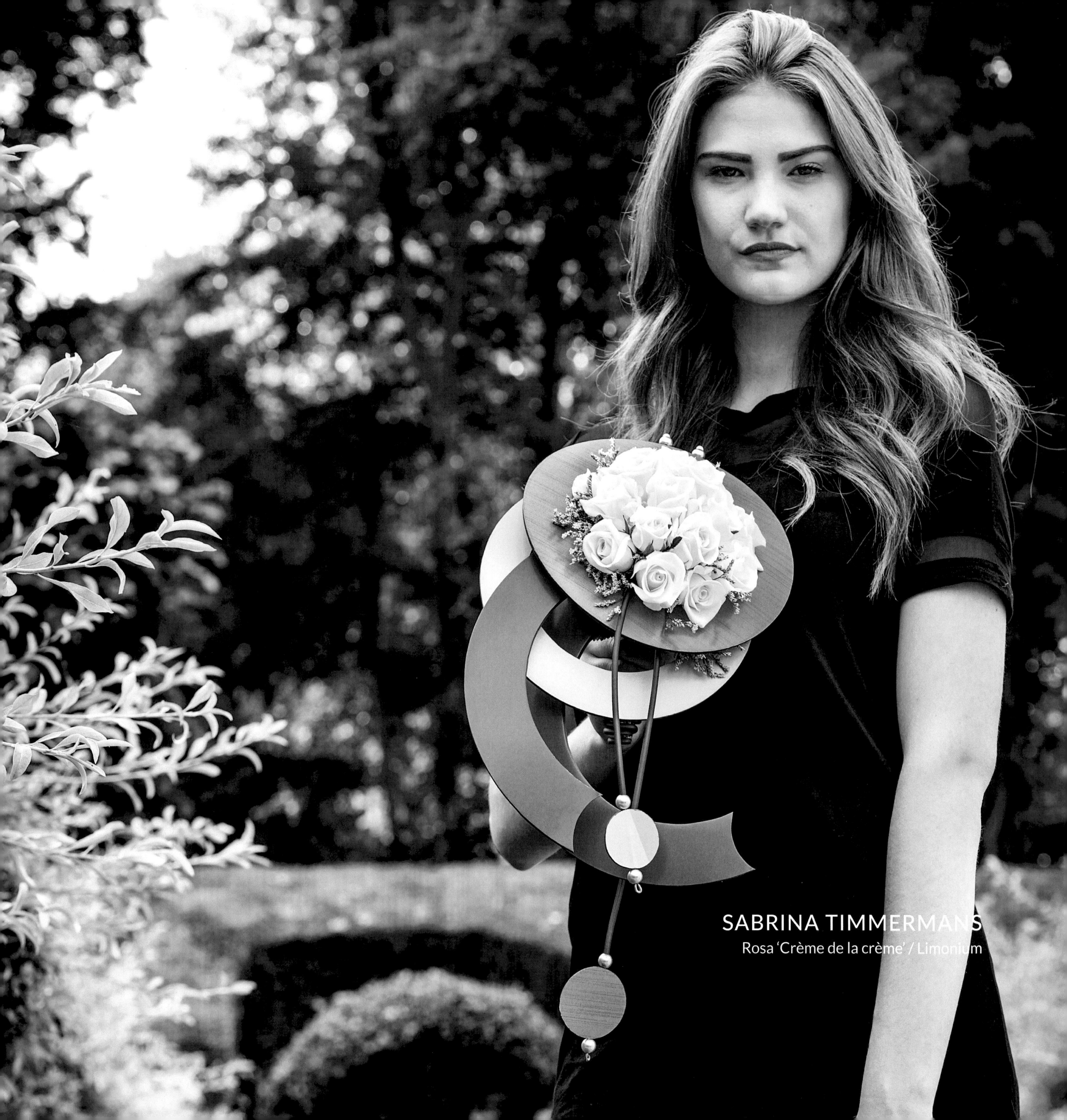

SABRINA TIMMERMANS
Rosa 'Crème de la crème' / Limonium

THE CIRCLE OF
LOVE

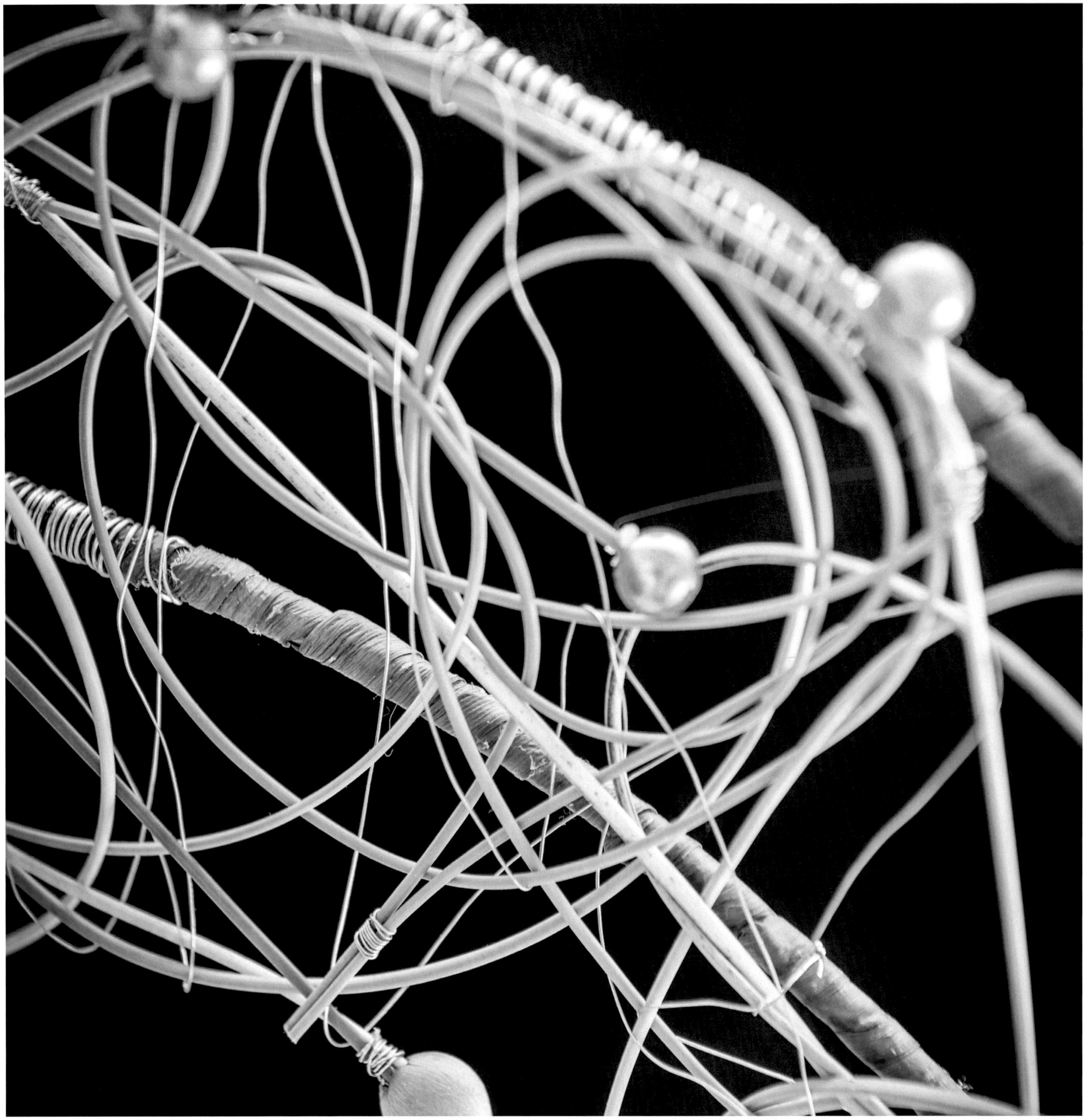

RIA BECKER

Phalaenopsis / Schoenus melanostachys (flexi grass) / Hypericum / Typha / Dianthus 'Green Trick'

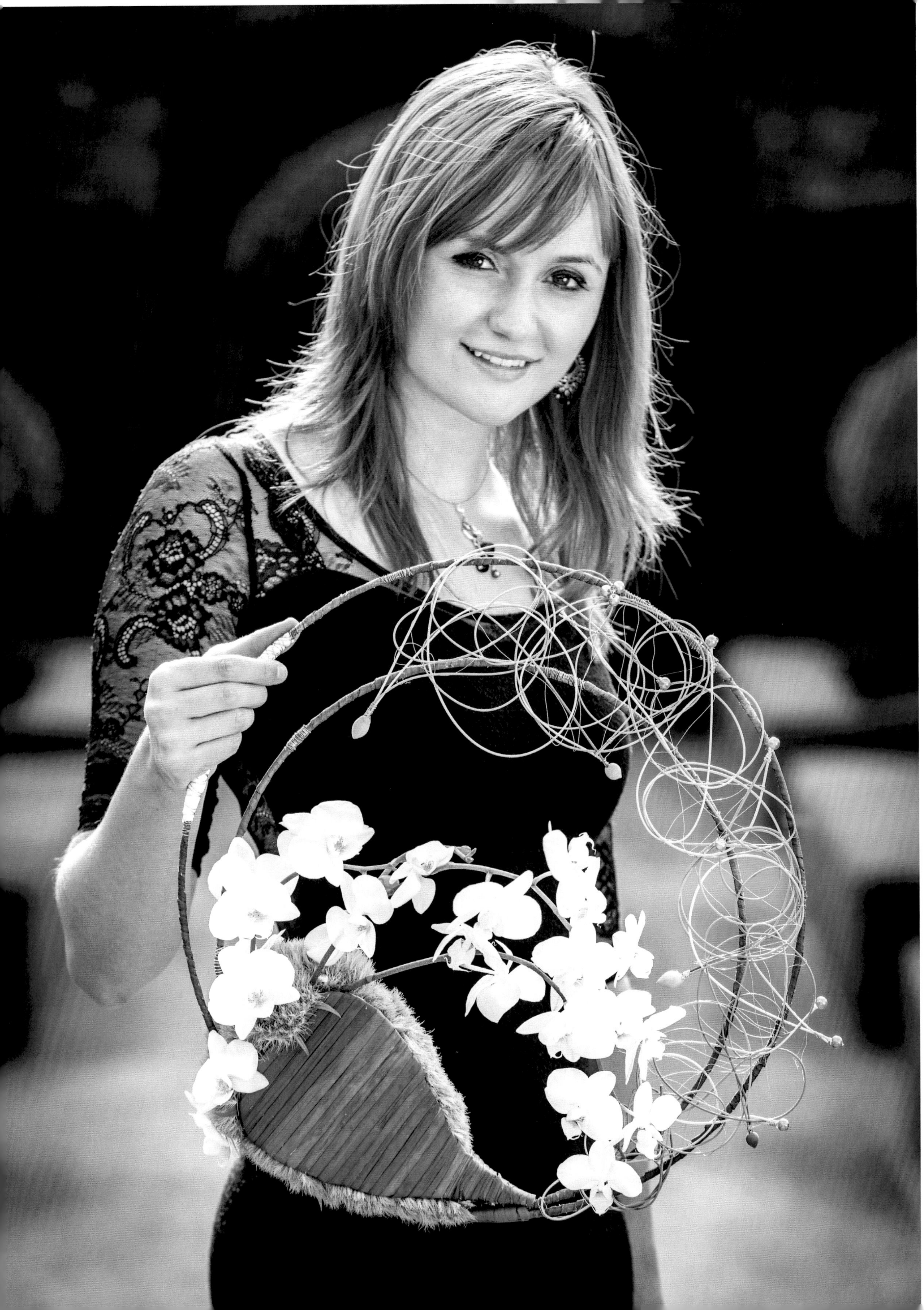

LAURENCE FONTAINE

Rosa / Phoenix

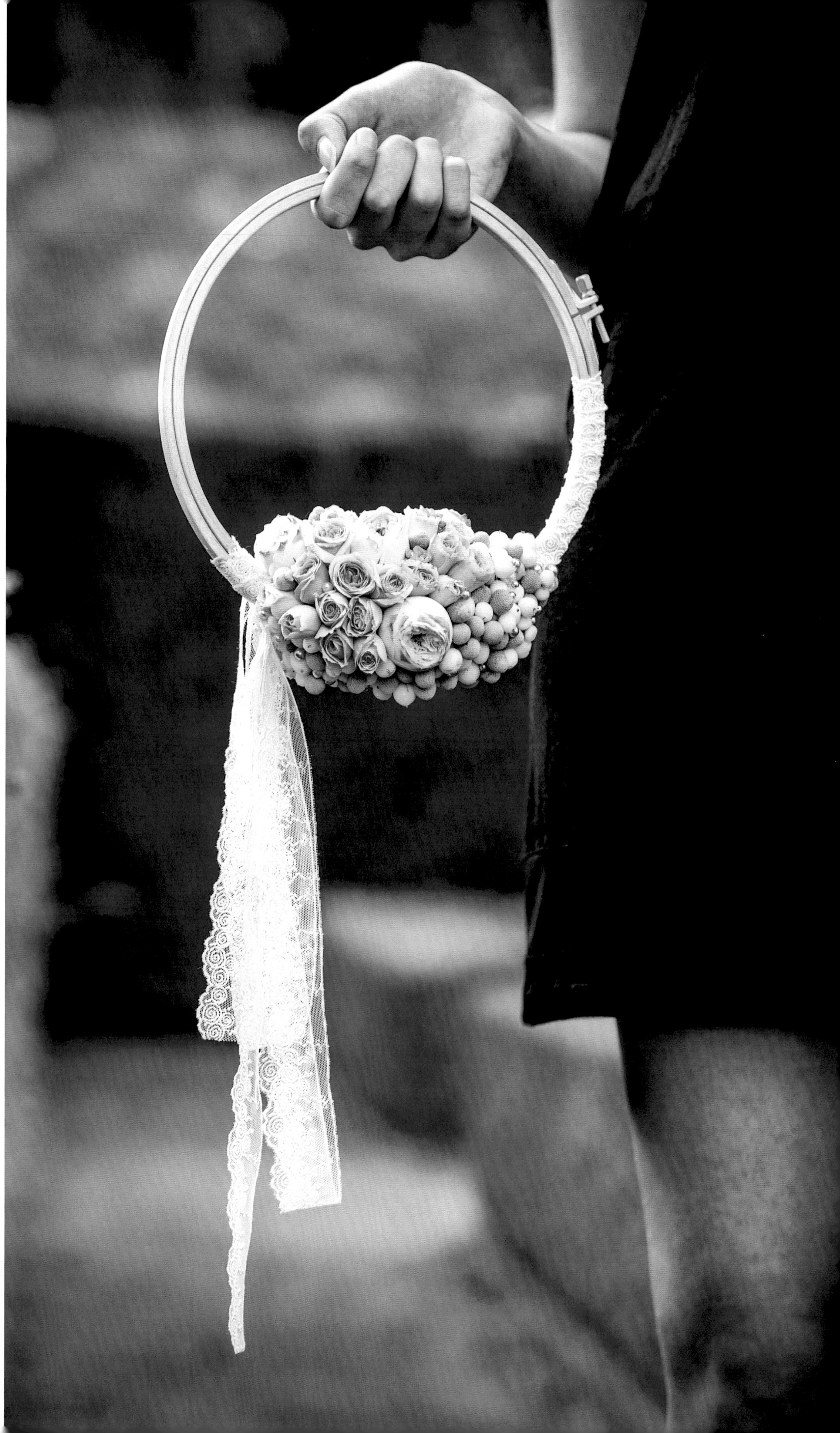

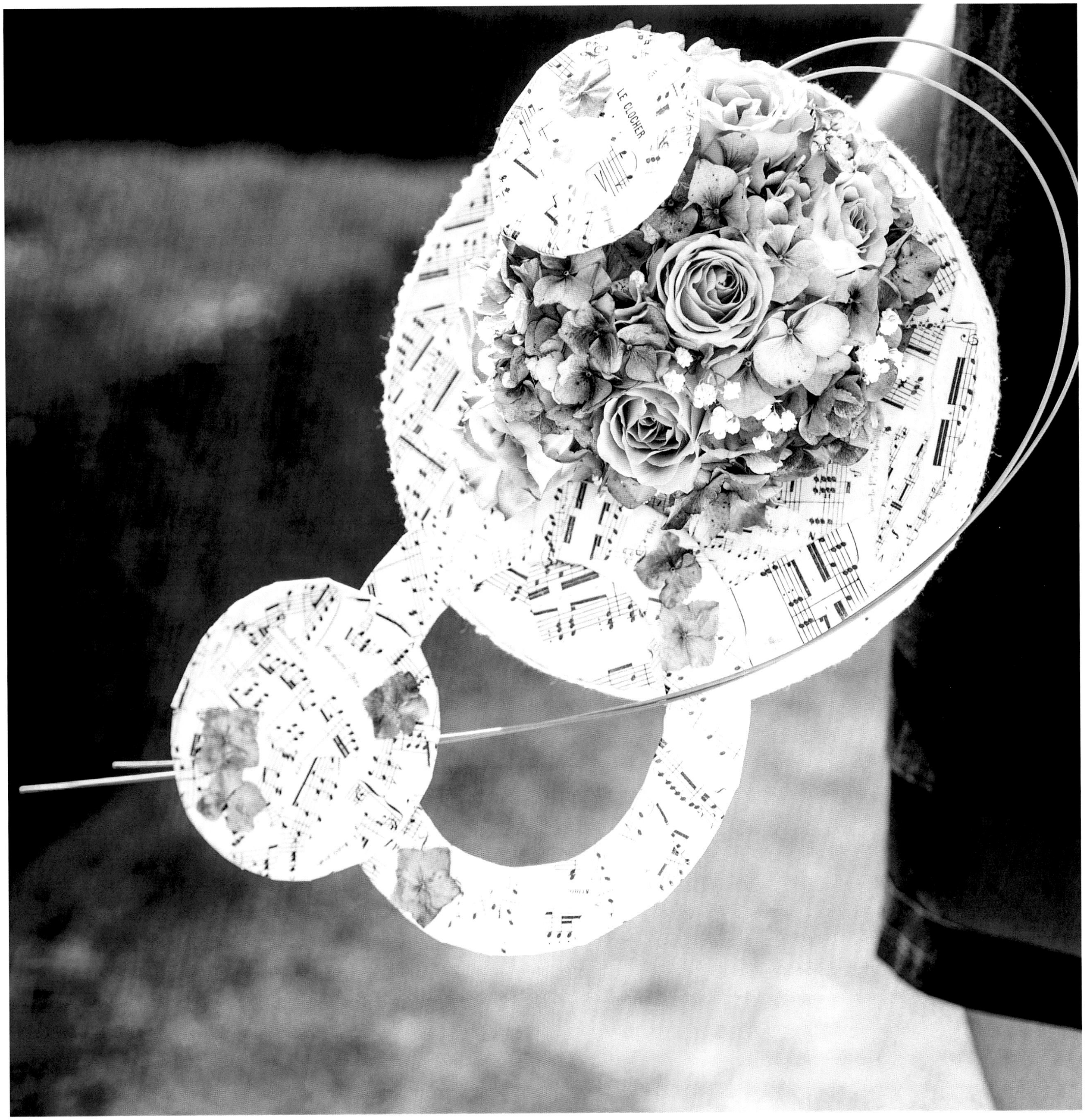

SÉBASTIEN DOSSIN

Hydrangea / Gypsophilla / Rosa / Schoenus melanostachys (flexi grass)

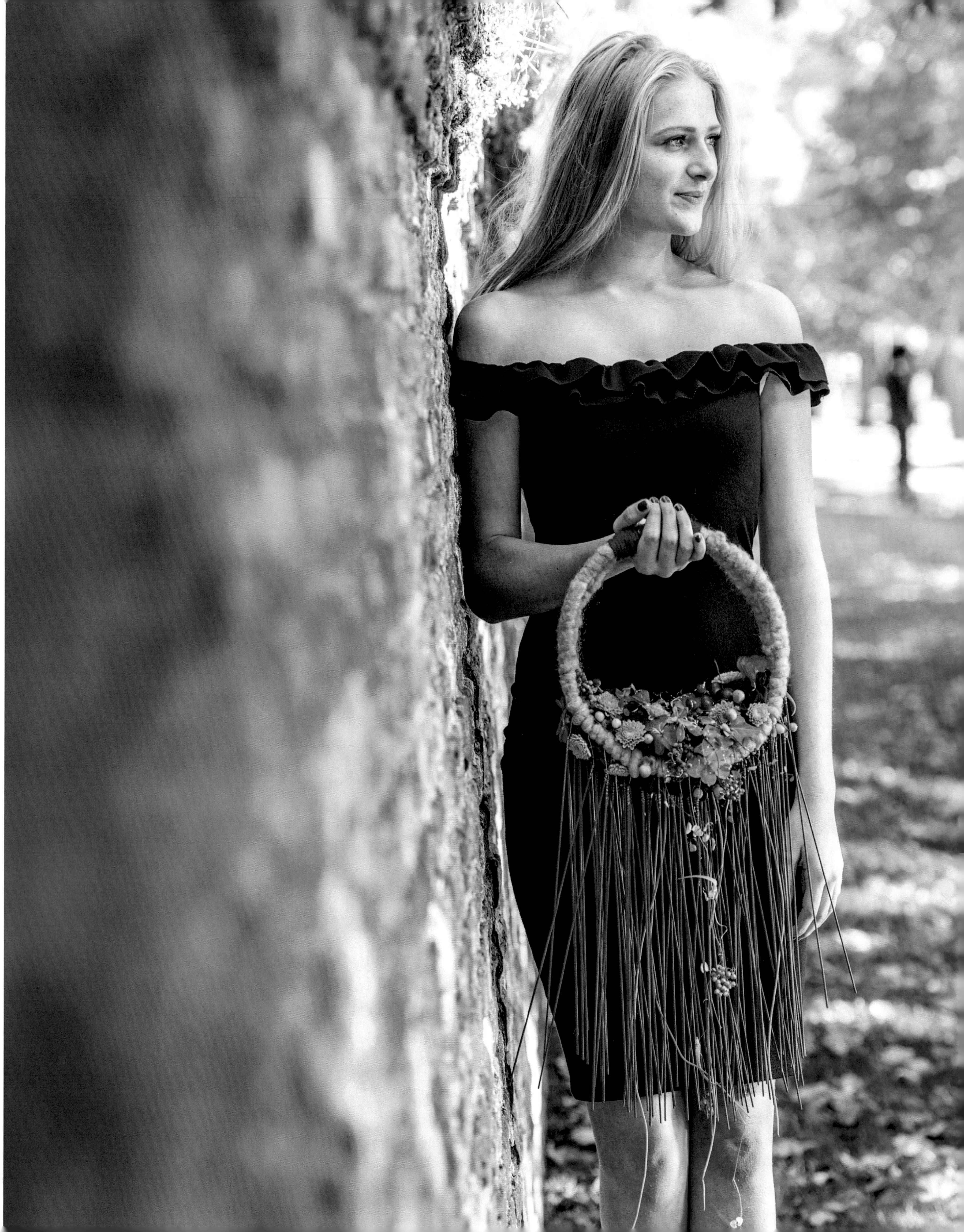

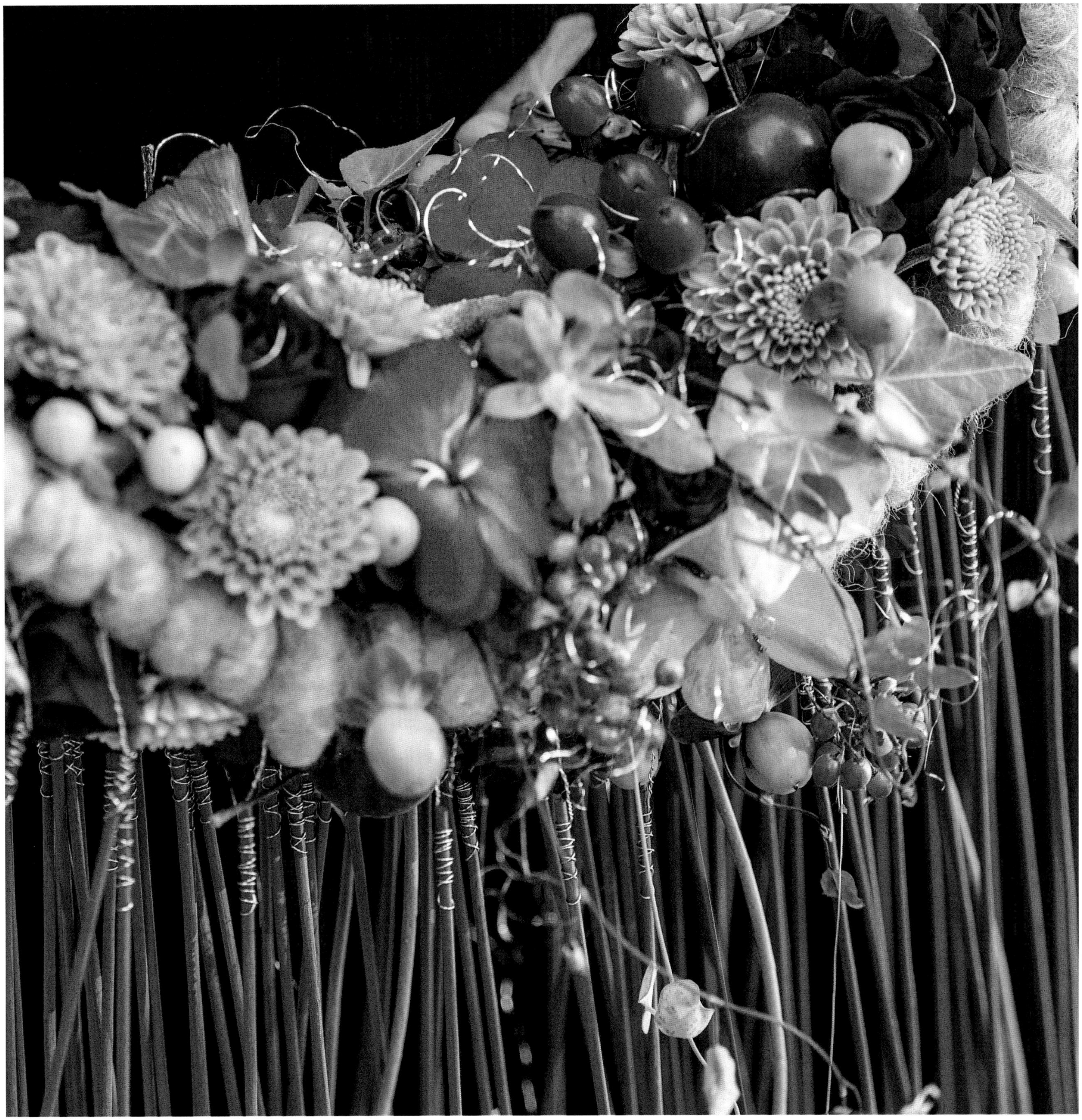

ILSE PALMAERS

Chrysanthemum / Hypericum inodorum / Dianthus / Vanda / Hedera helix / Rosa / Malus / Rhipsalis / Muehlenbeckia

POWERFUL
CREATIVE

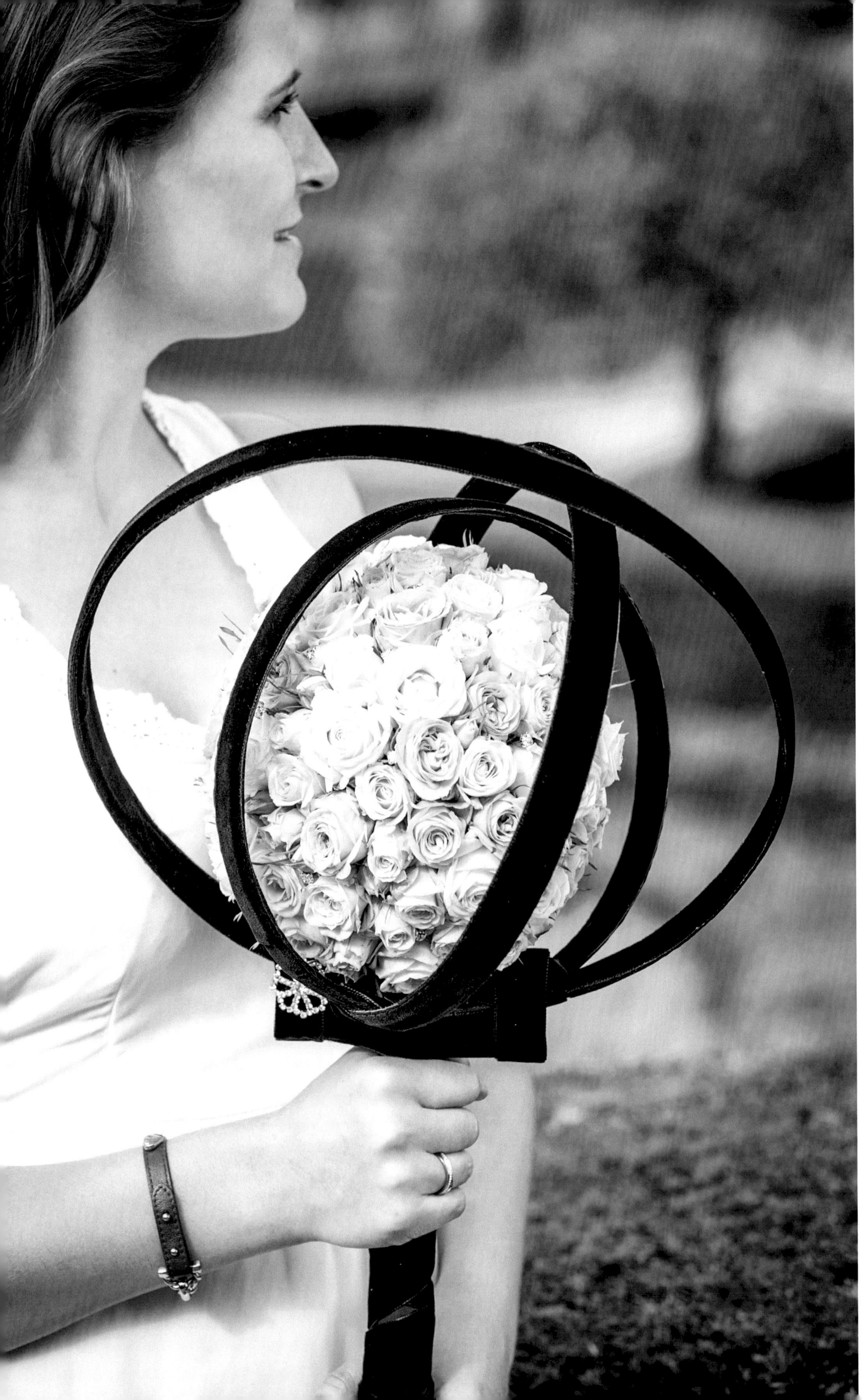

SÉBASTIEN DOSSIN
Rosa

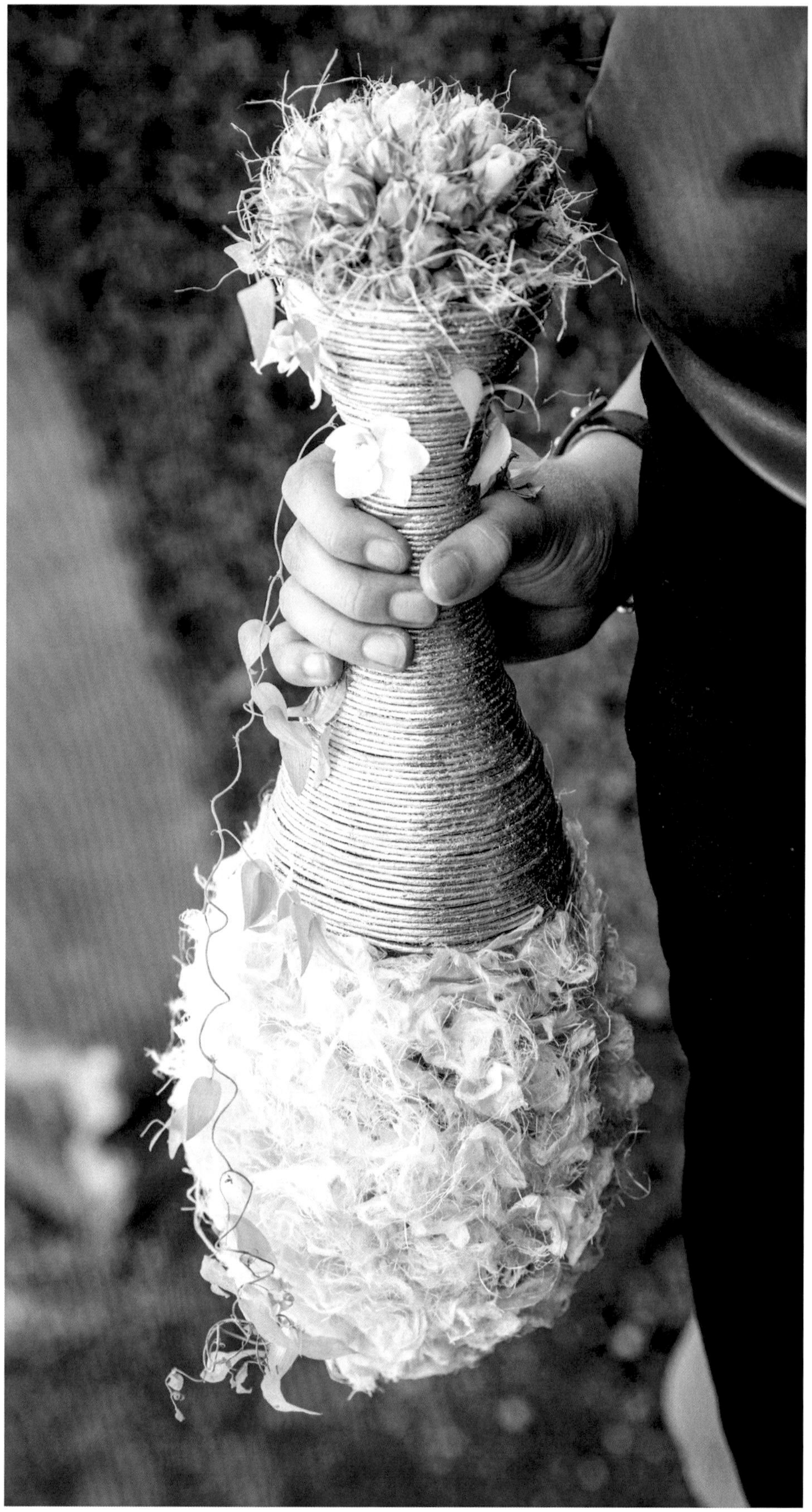

ILSE PALMAERS

Rosa
Tillandsia usneoides
Asparagus asparagoides
Phalaenopsis

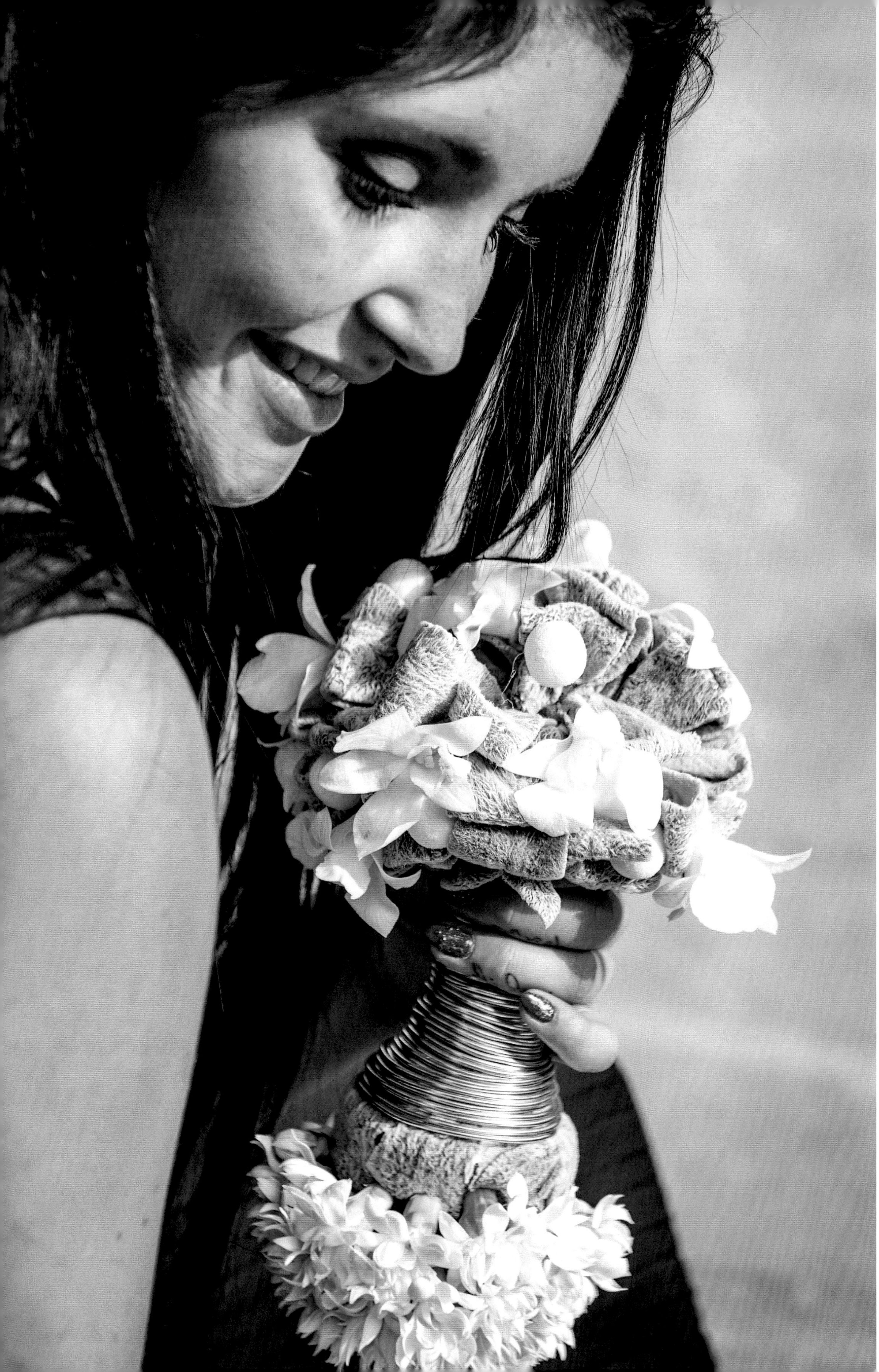

MARTINE
DESSY

Dianthus 'Tros Star'

Stachys

Dendrobium

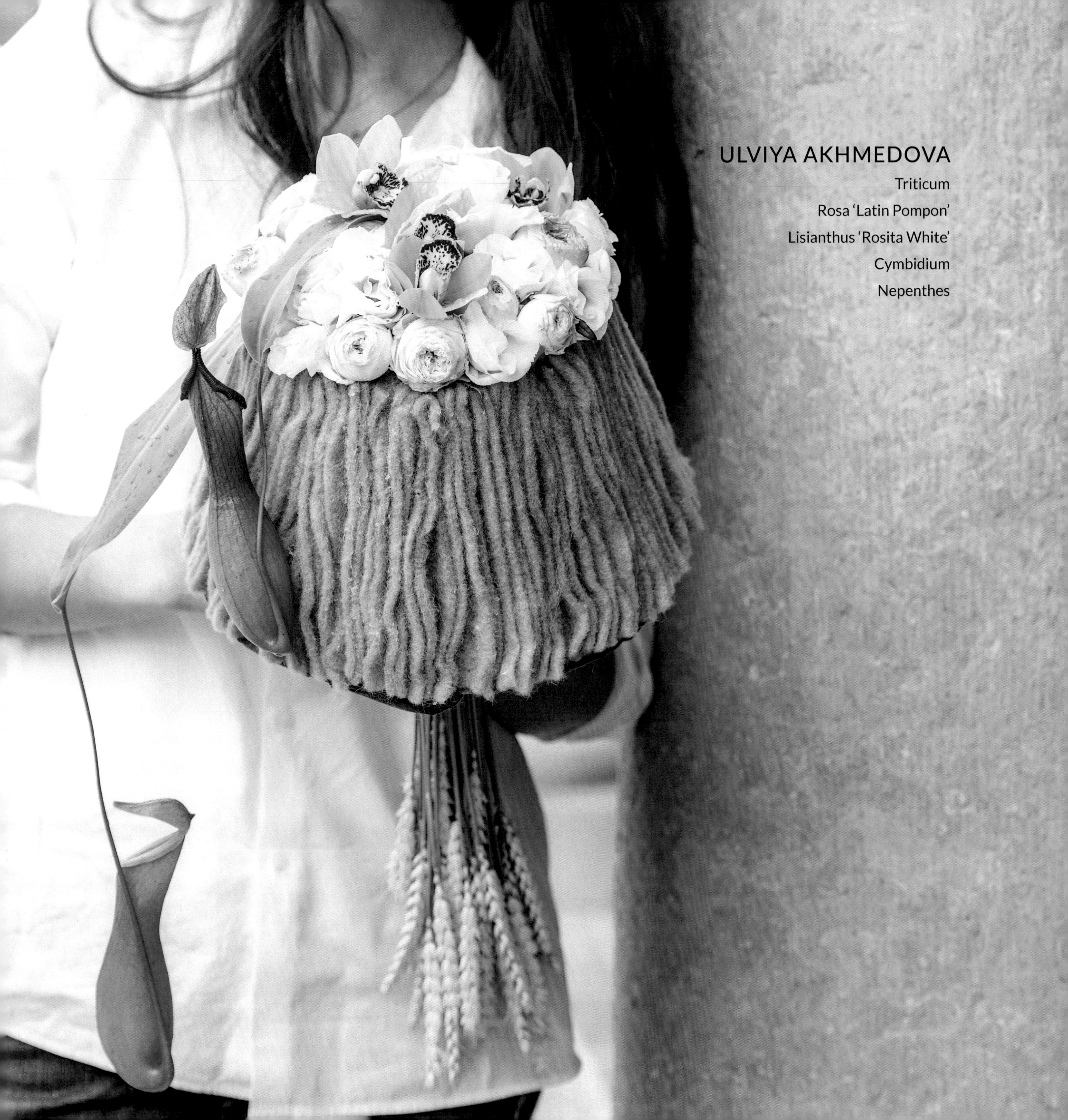

ULVIYA AKHMEDOVA

Triticum

Rosa 'Latin Pompon'

Lisianthus 'Rosita White'

Cymbidium

Nepenthes

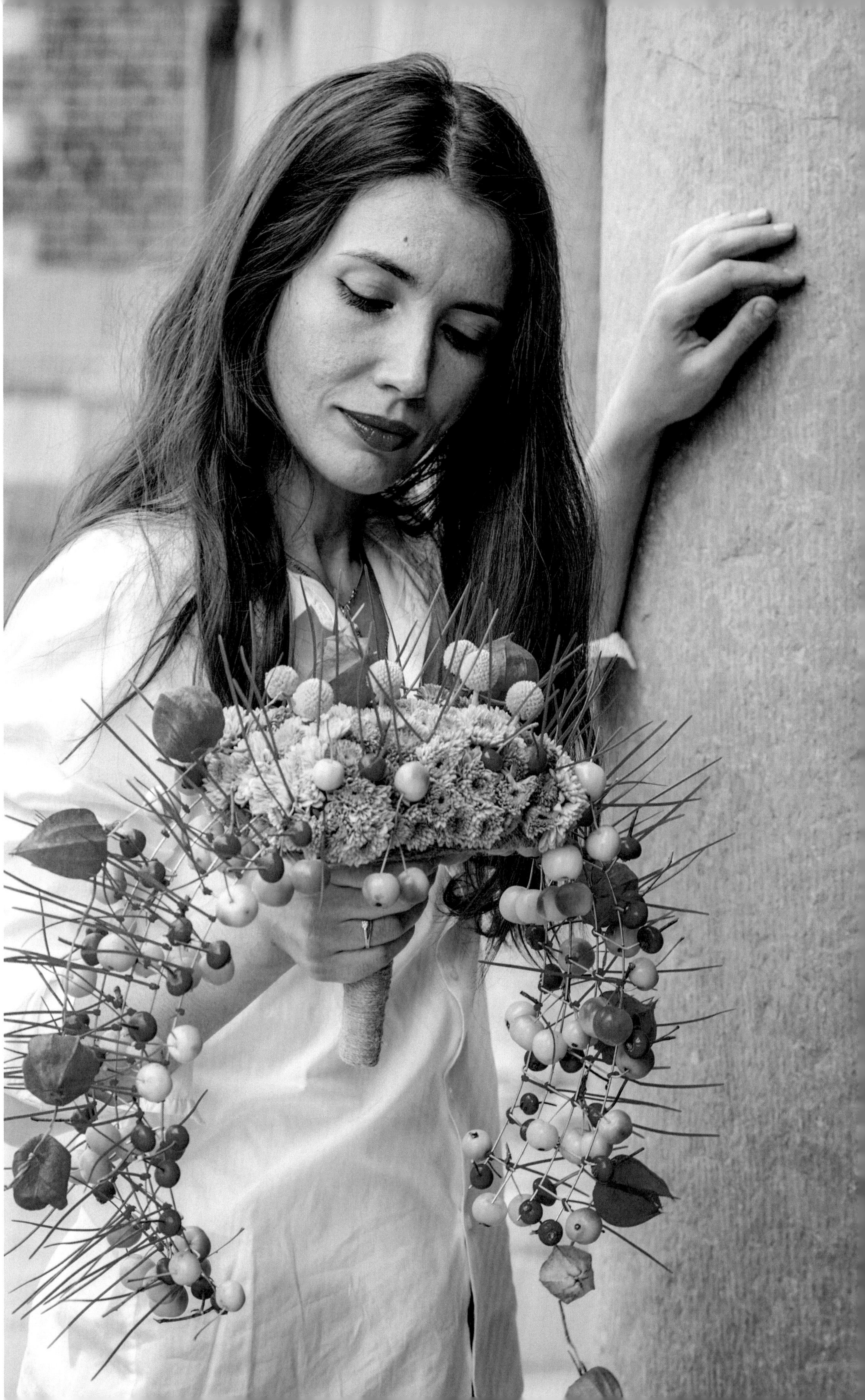

ULVIYA AKHMEDOVA

Chrysanthemum Santini 'Jeanny Peach'
Craspedia
Malus
Physalis

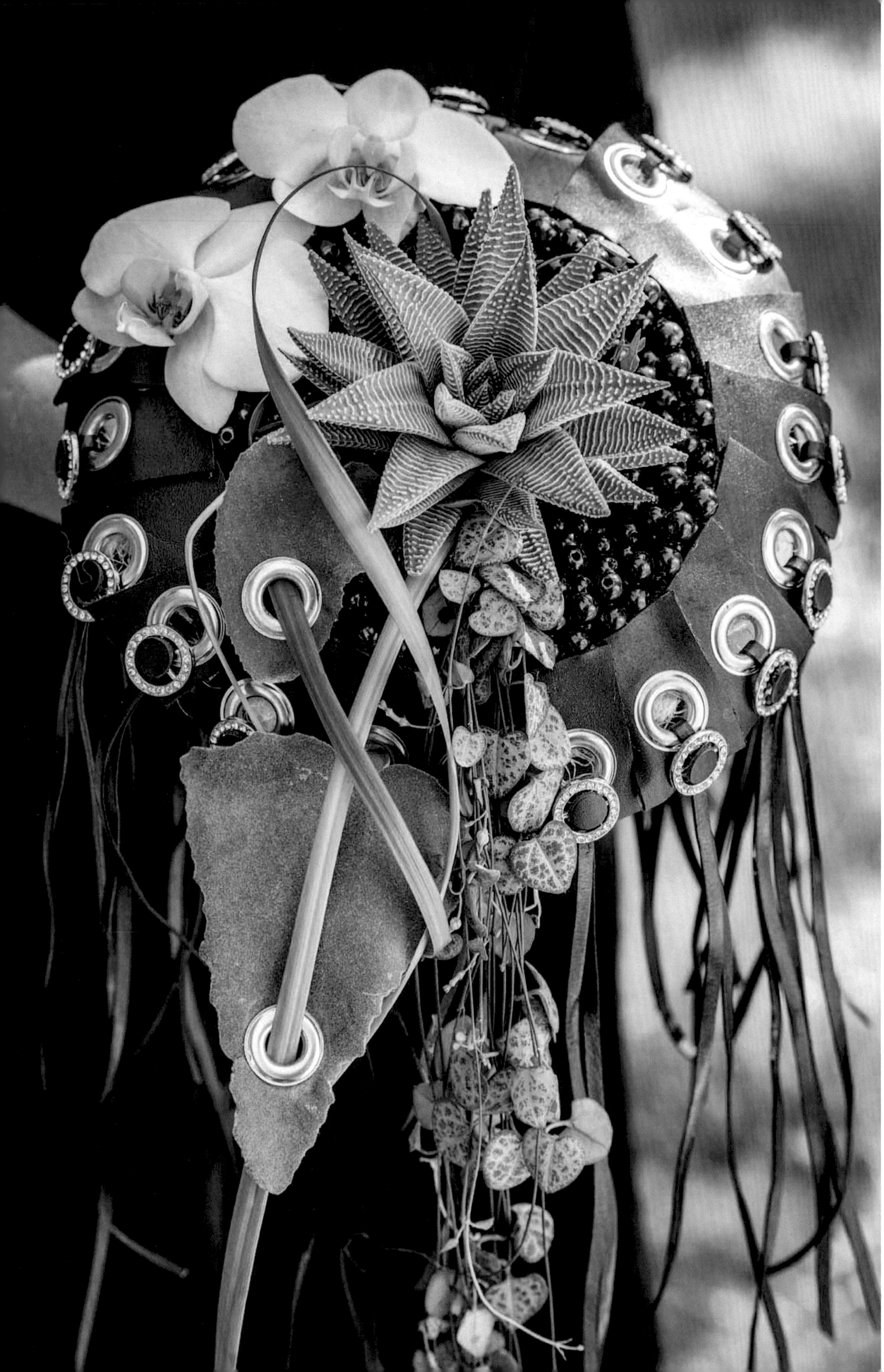

PIRJO KOPPI

Phalaenopsis
Kalanchoe beharensis
Ceropegia woodii
Lily grass
Haworthia pumila

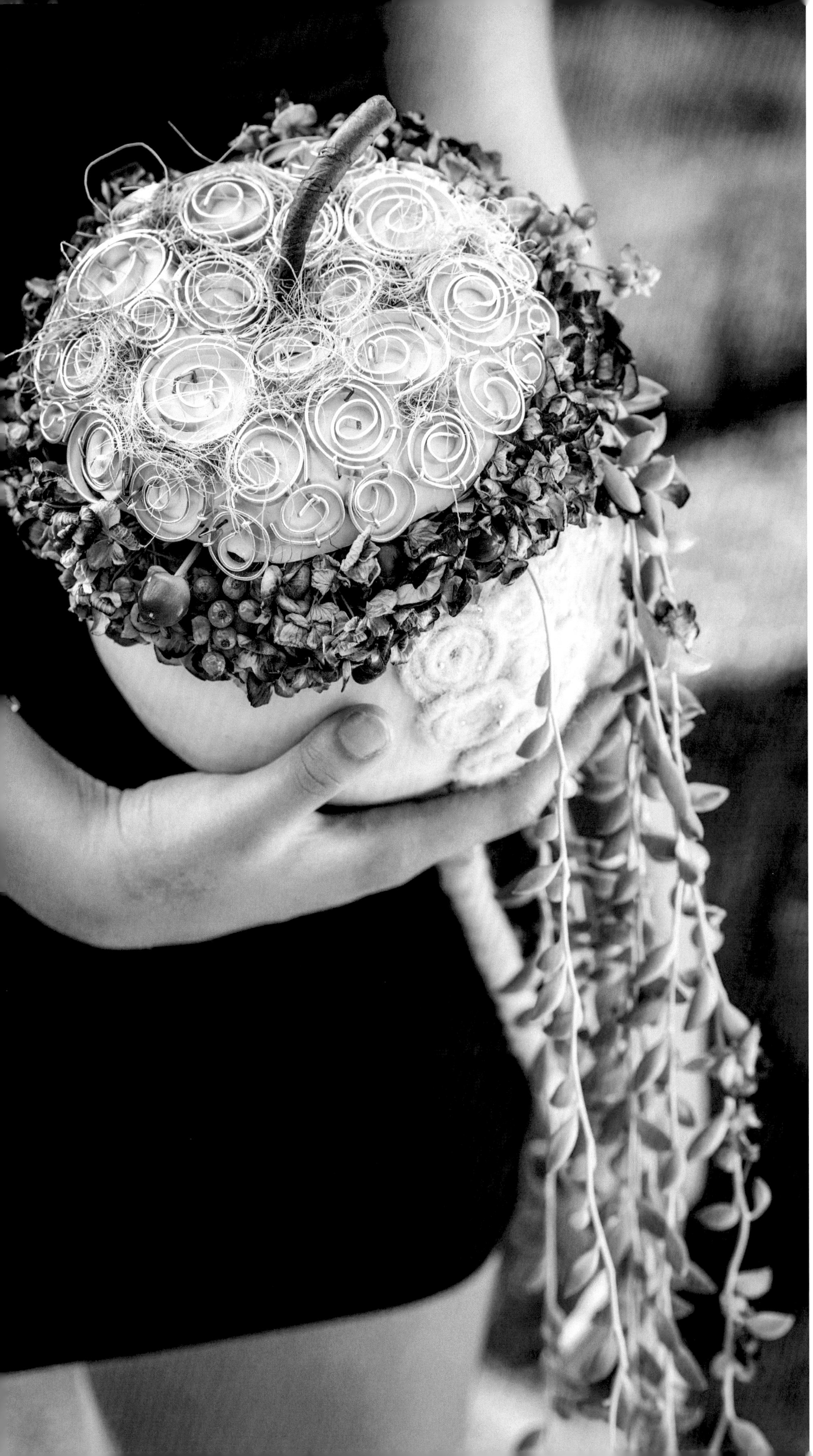

ELS VUYLSTEKE

Hydrangea

Rosa, rose hips

Hypericum

Senecio

36

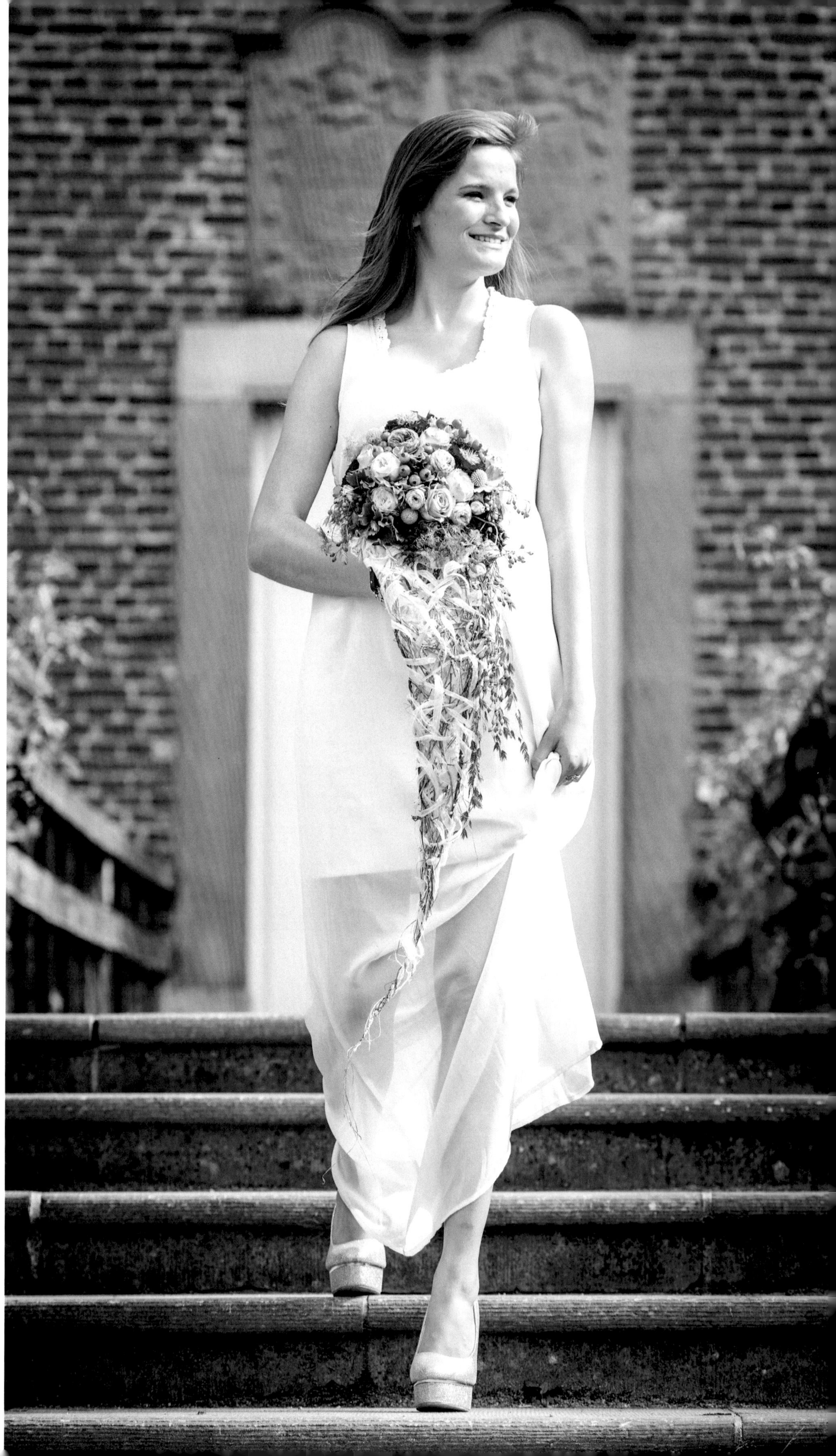

ADINDA SAP

Rosa 'Piano'
Rosa 'Lavender'
Rosa 'Ivanhoe'
Dahlia
Cotinus
Rosa, rose hips
Hydrangea
Carex
Craspedia
Dianthus
Briza
Euonymus
Morus

OUR LOVE
IS LIKE A
WATERFALL

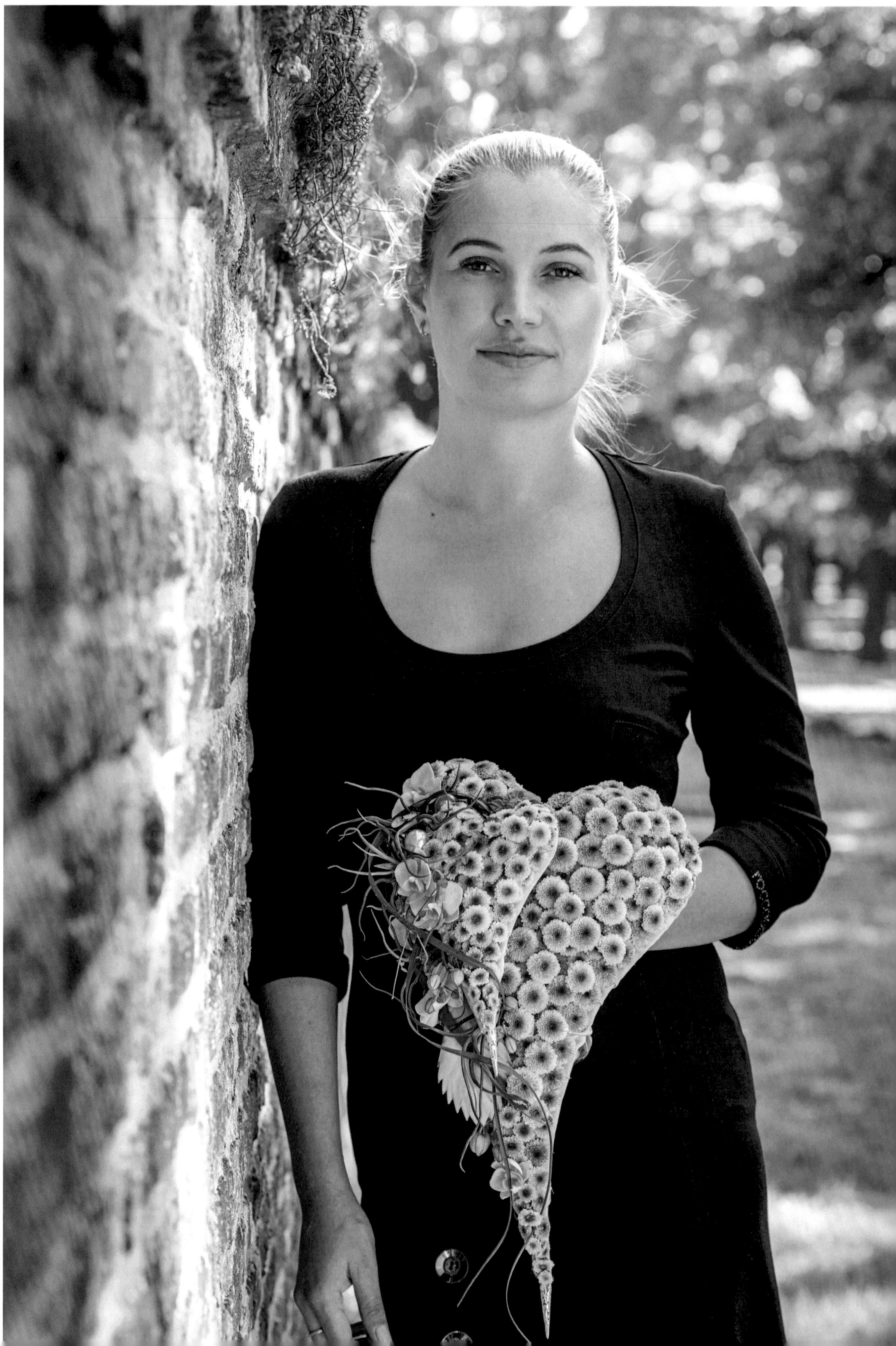

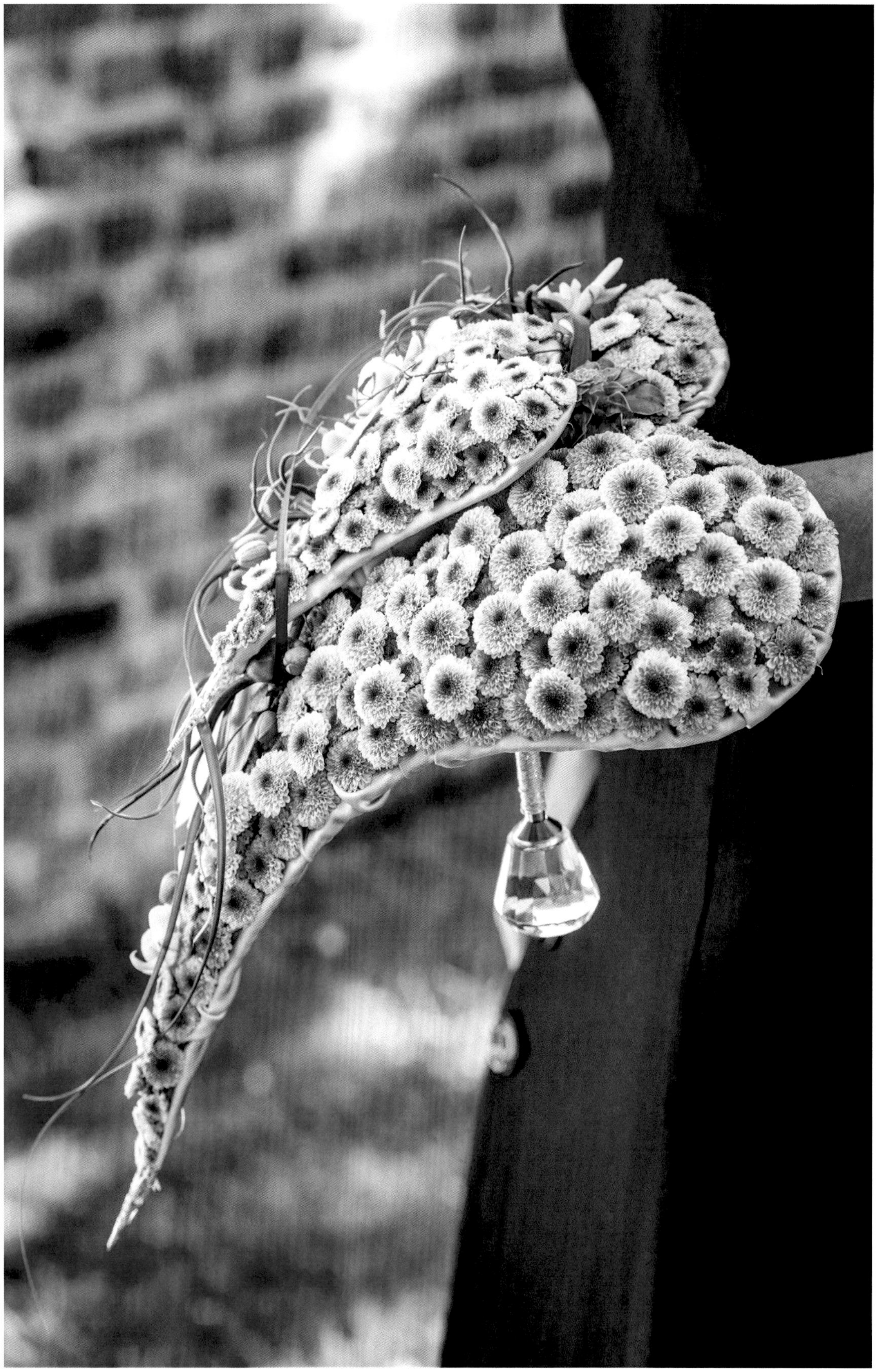

PIRJO KOPPI

Chrysanthemum Santini / Phalaenopsis / Ceropegia woodii / Tillandsia cyanea / Echeveria

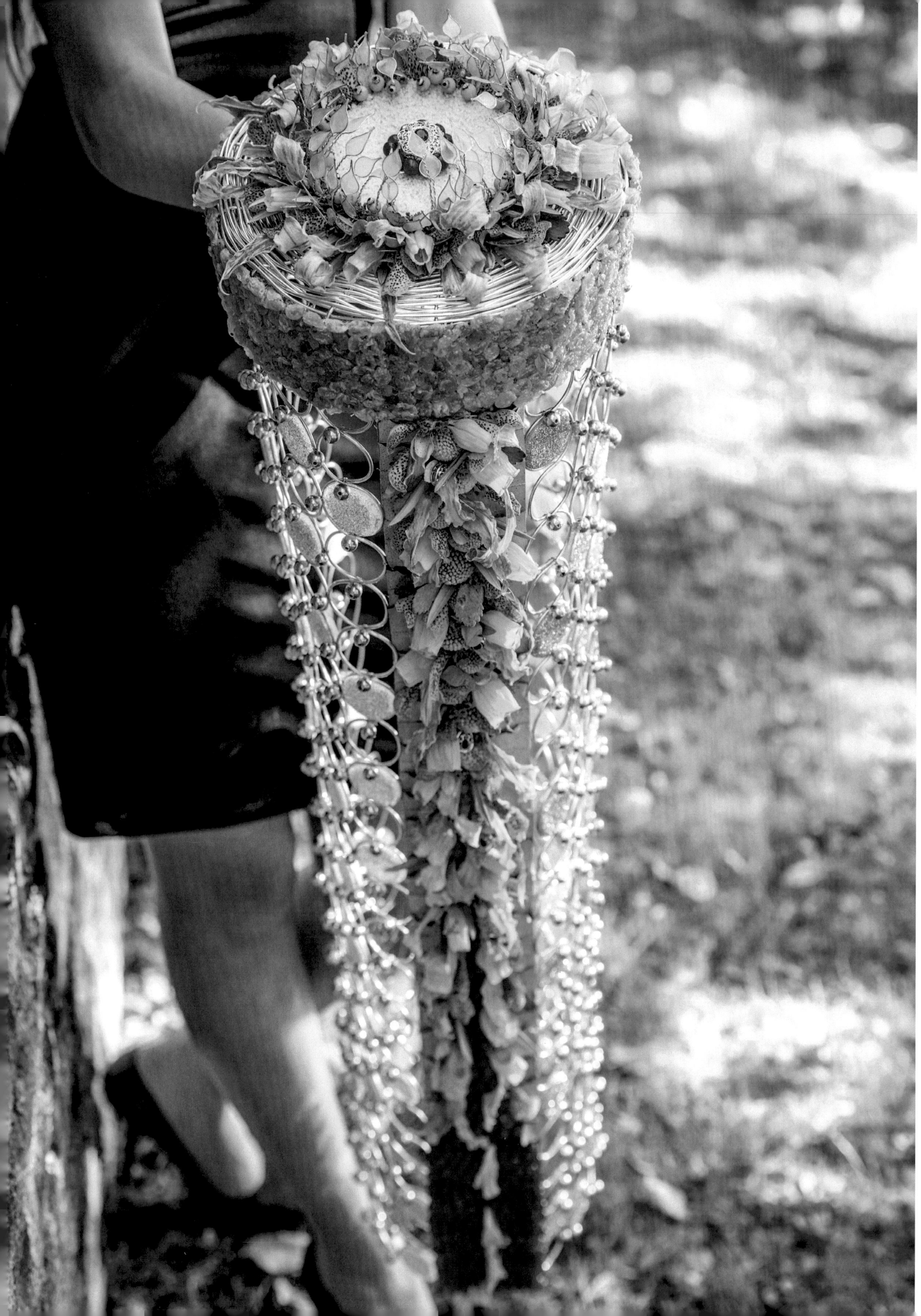

EMILIE
BOUDONNET

Rosa, rose hips

Sandersonia

Craspedia

Asclepias

Virburnum opulus berries

Echeveria

Vitis vinifera 'Korinthiaka', dried fruit

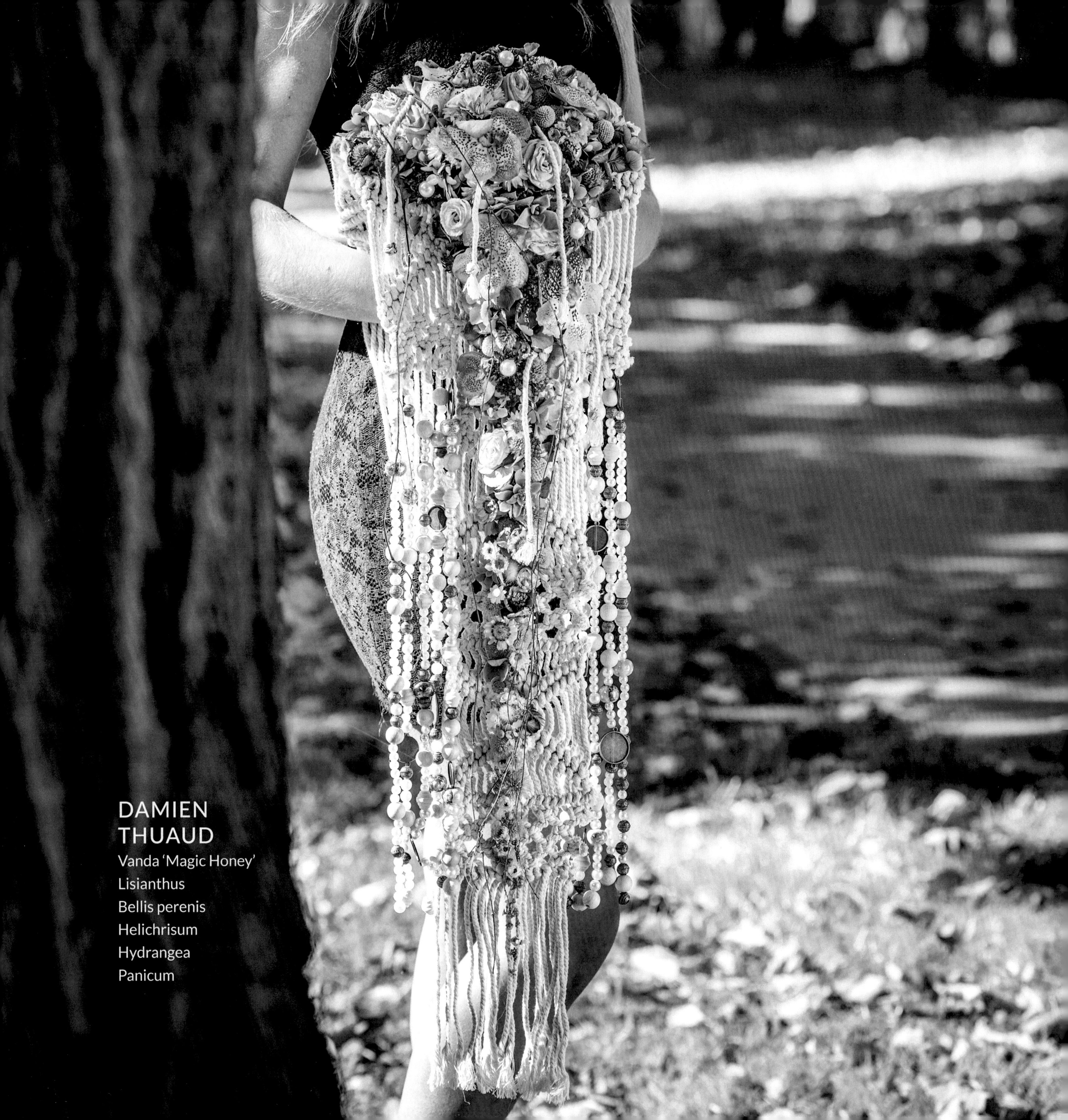

DAMIEN THUAUD

Vanda 'Magic Honey'
Lisianthus
Bellis perenis
Helichrisum
Hydrangea
Panicum

"HAPPILY EVER AFTER"

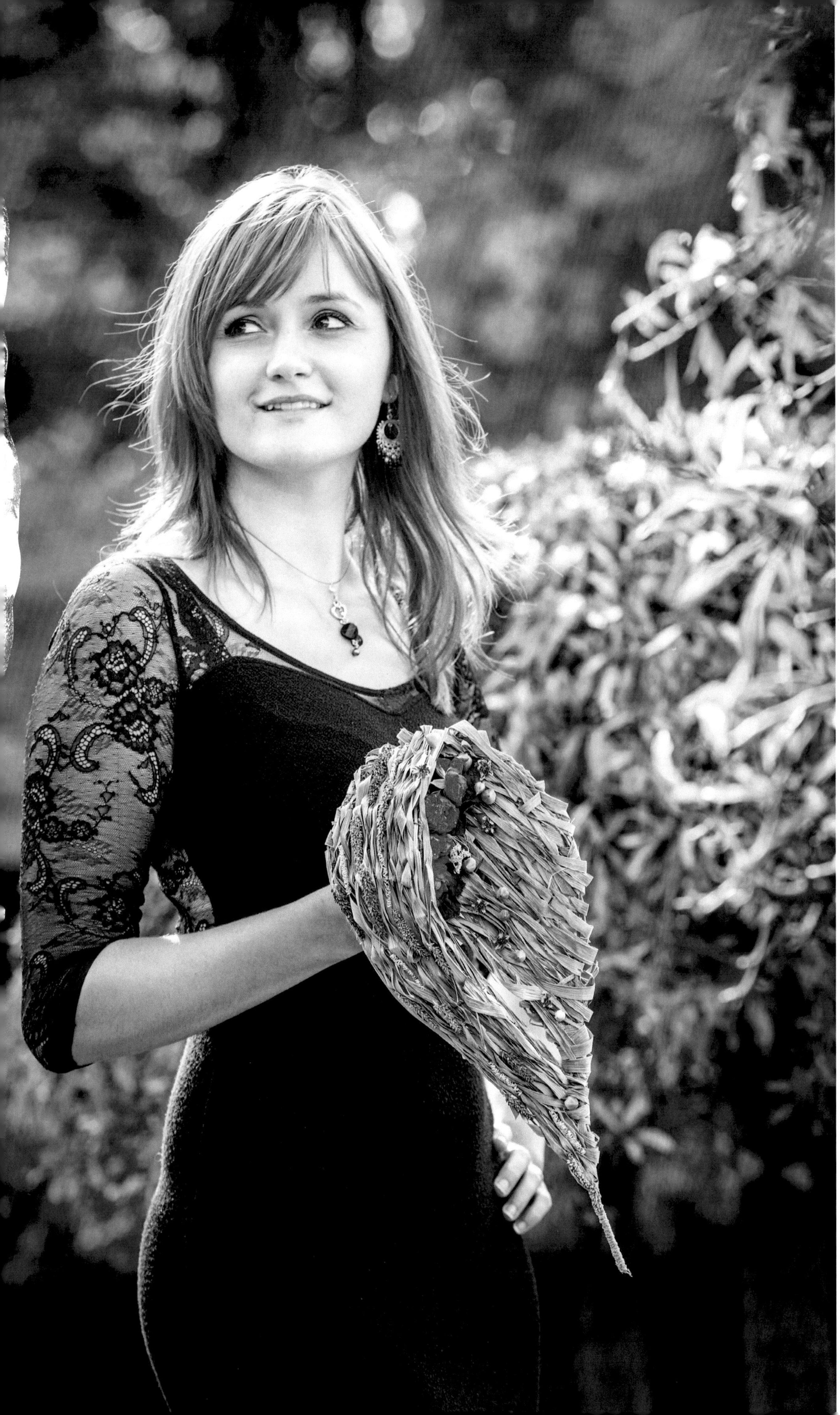

VIKTORIA NOPPEN
Miscanthus floridulus
Hypericum 'Magical Desire'
Borago officinalis
Alchemilla mollis

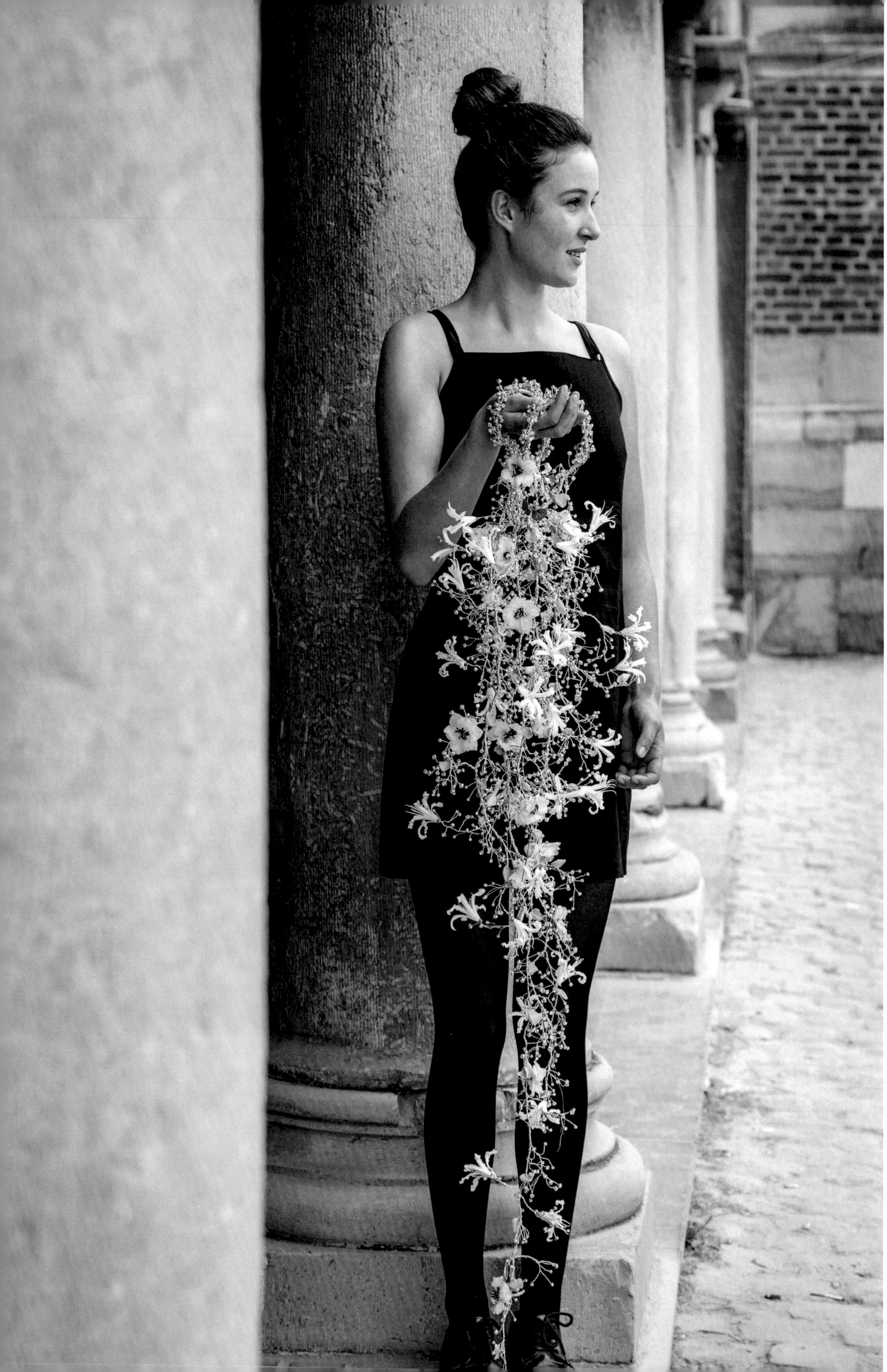

SÖREN VAN LAER

Helleborus
Nerine
Delphinium
Ceropegia woodii

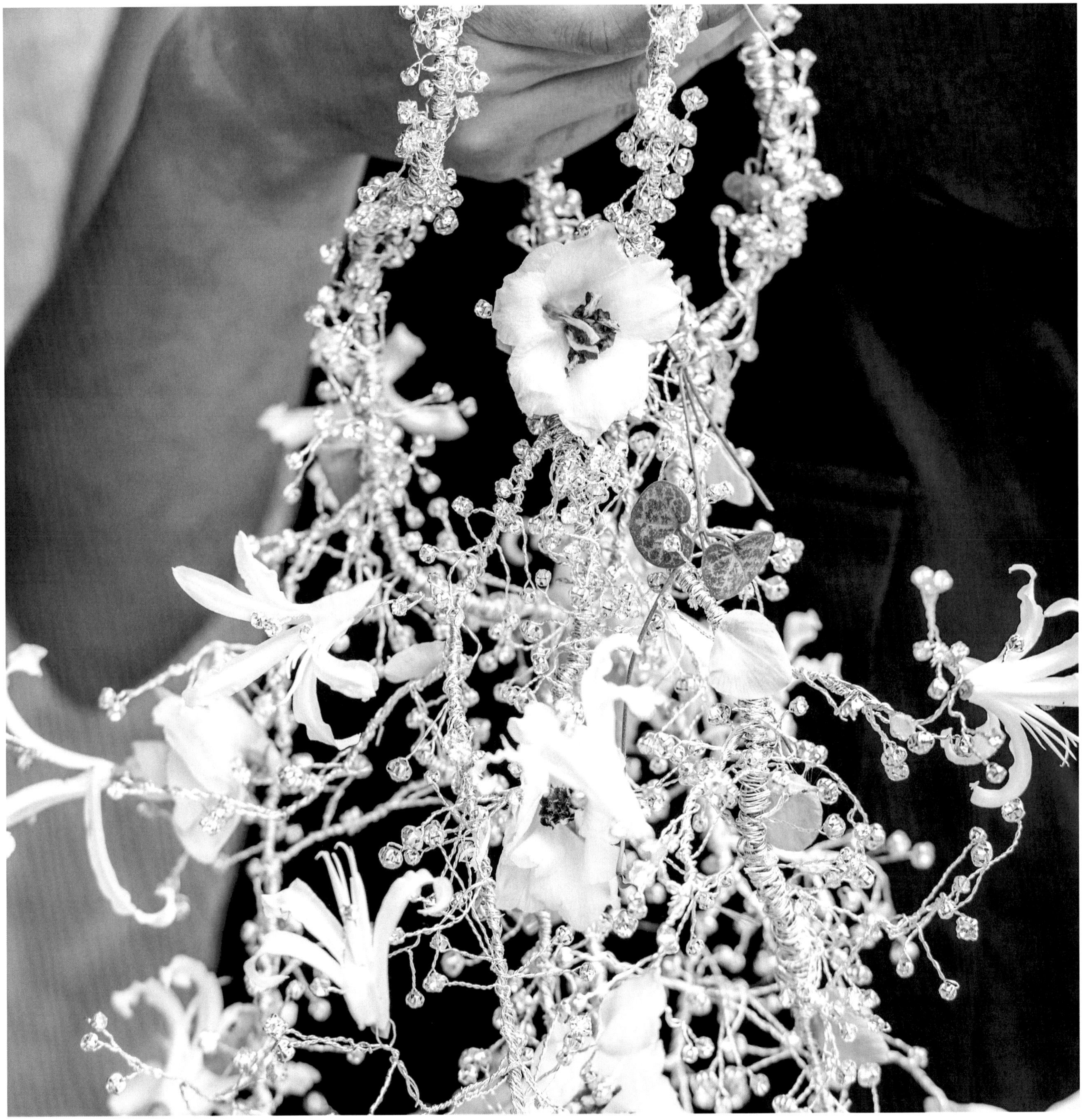

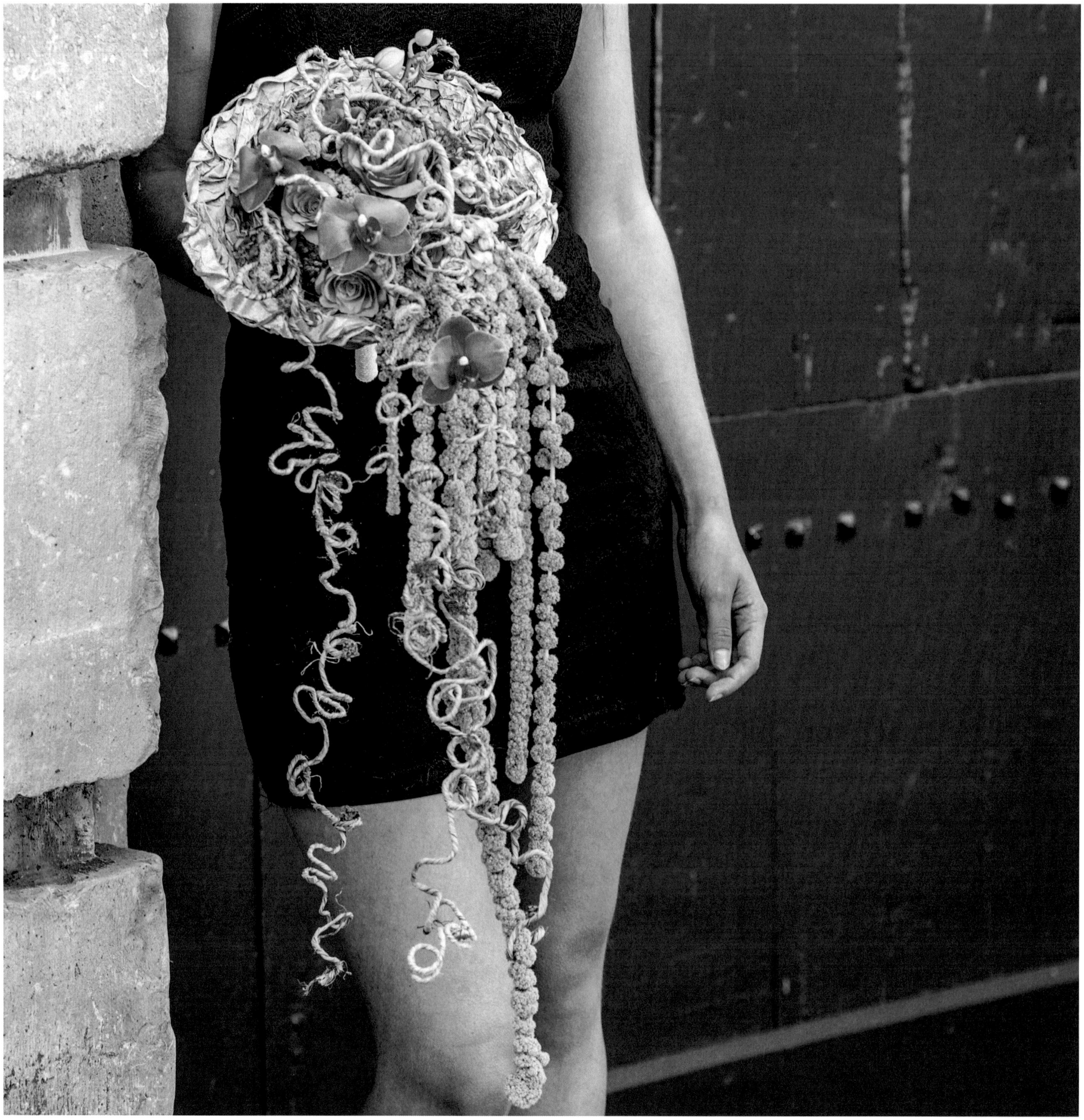

ELS GEERDENS

Rosa / Sedum / Phalaenopsis / Leonotis leonurus / Amaranthus

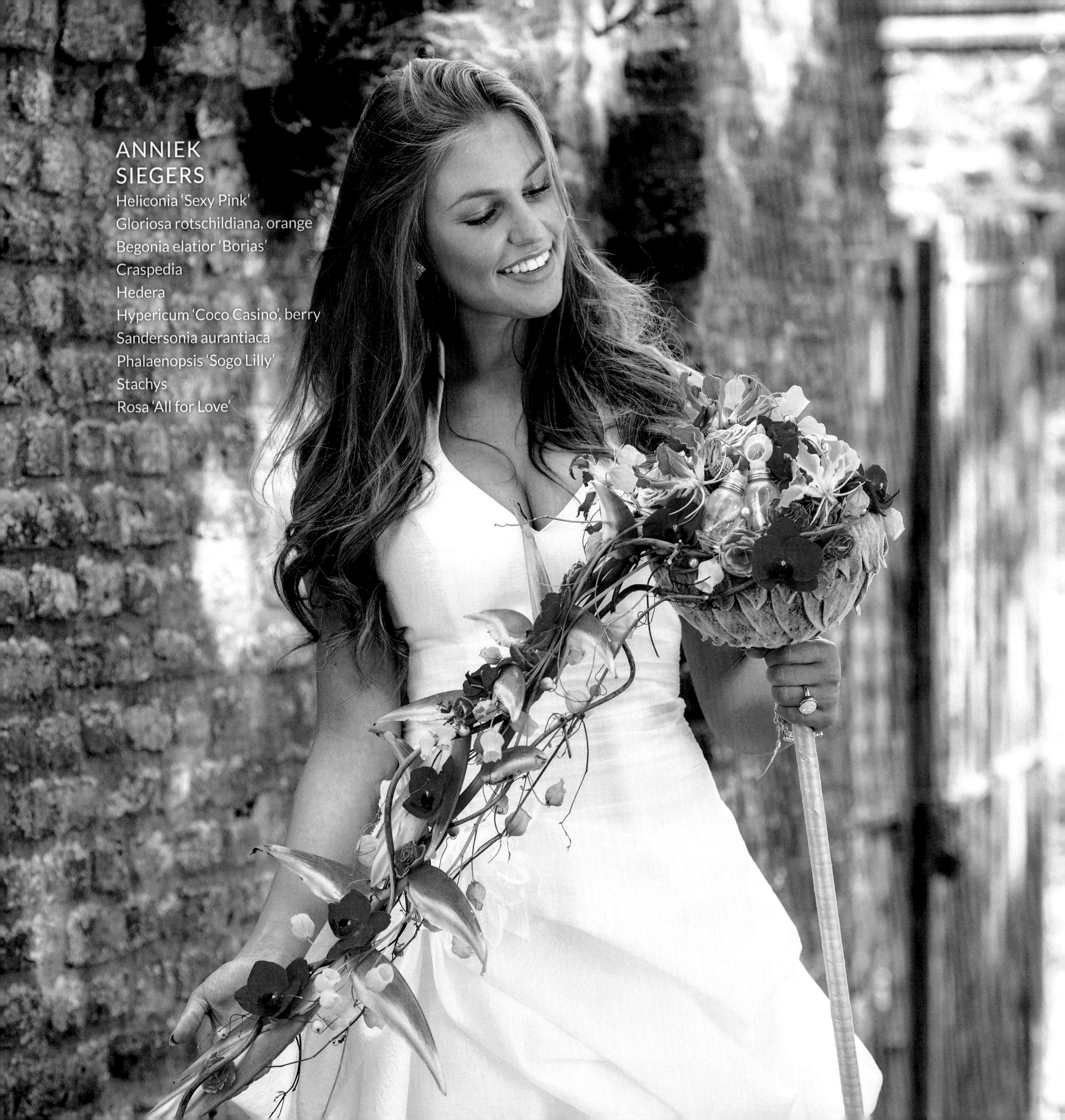

ANNIEK SIEGERS

Heliconia 'Sexy Pink'
Gloriosa rotschildiana, orange
Begonia elatior 'Borias'
Craspedia
Hedera
Hypericum 'Coco Casino', berry
Sandersonia aurantiaca
Phalaenopsis 'Sogo Lilly'
Stachys
Rosa 'All for Love'

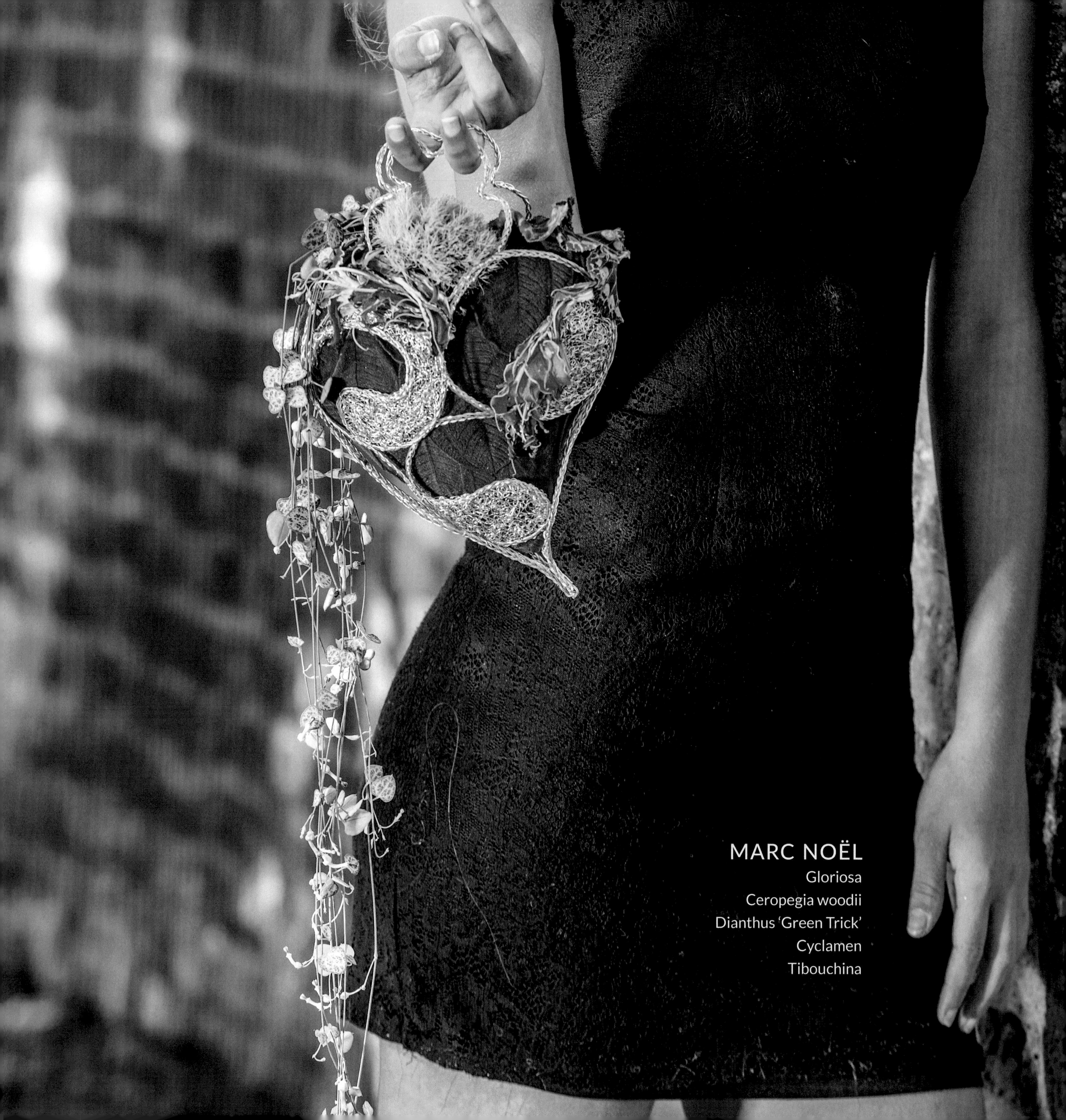

MARC NOËL

Gloriosa
Ceropegia woodii
Dianthus 'Green Trick'
Cyclamen
Tibouchina

POWERFUL
FLOWER
PURSE

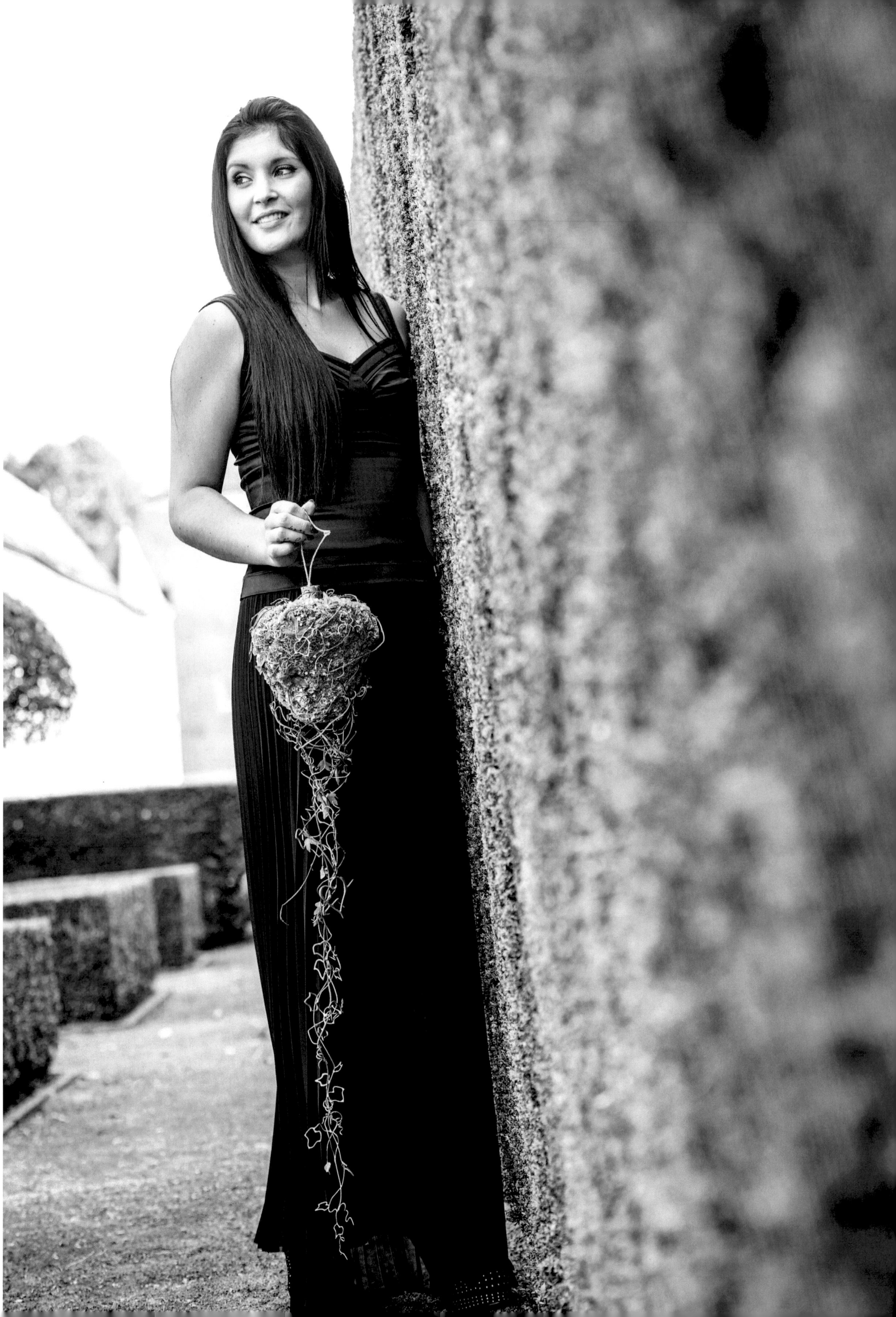

NESS
KLOROFYL
Limonium sinuatum

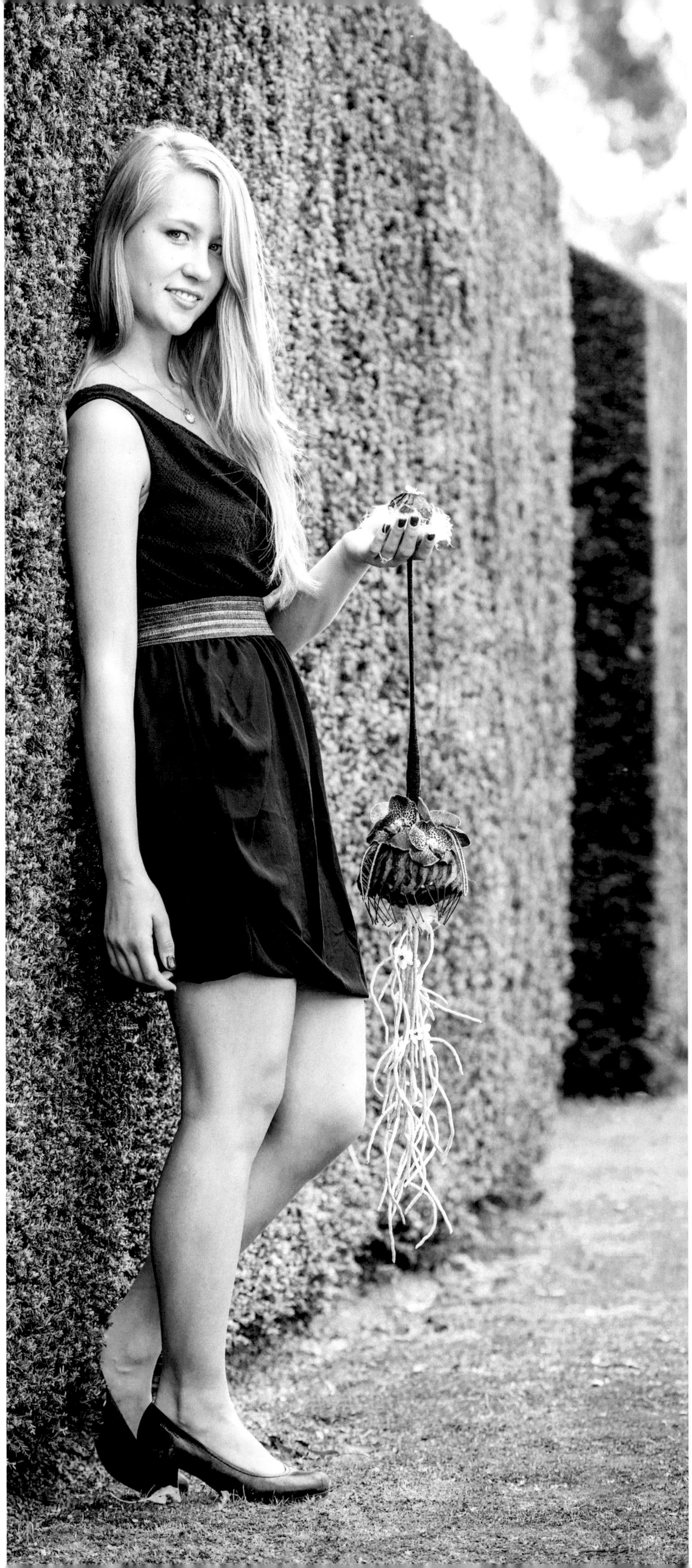

JOLIEN VANDERSTAPPEN

Cotinus

Vanda 'Black Magic'

Vanda roots

Clematis

Ornithogalum arabicum

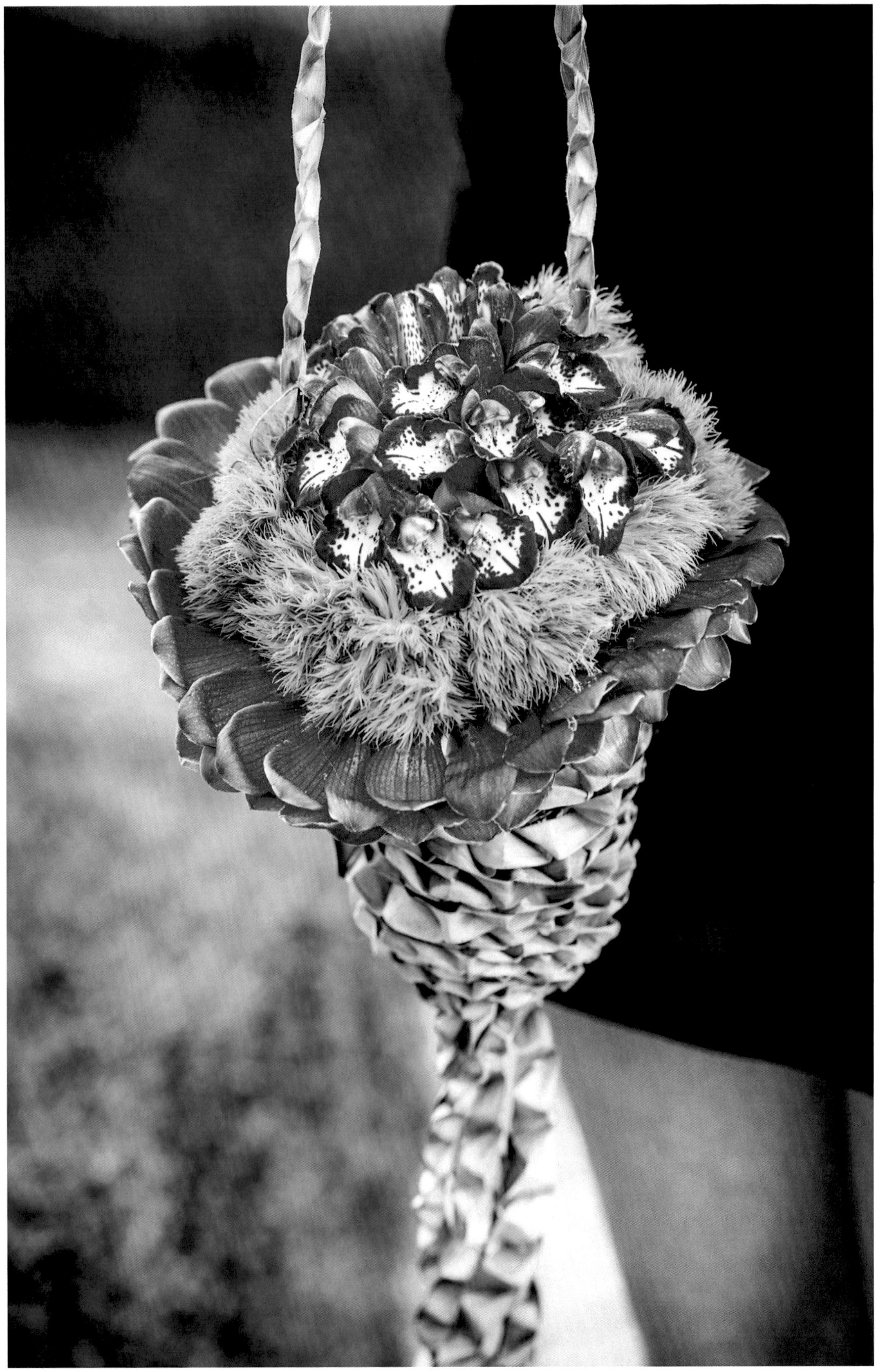

INEKE TURANGAN

Cymbidium / Dianthus 'Green Trick' / Cocos, coconut leafs

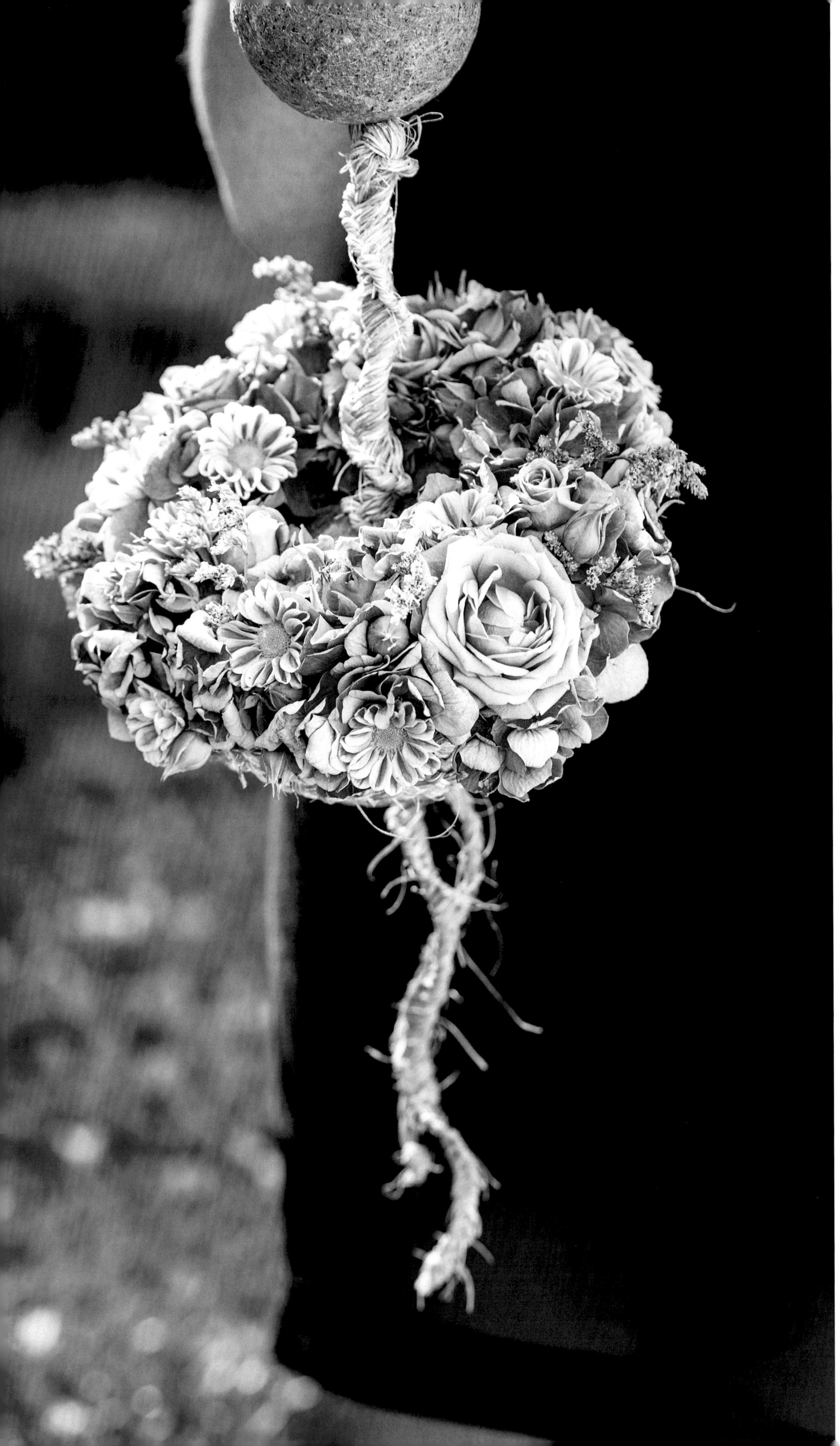

EBRINA DIELEMAN

Hydrangea
Chrysanthemum
Rosa
Limonium
Typha

54

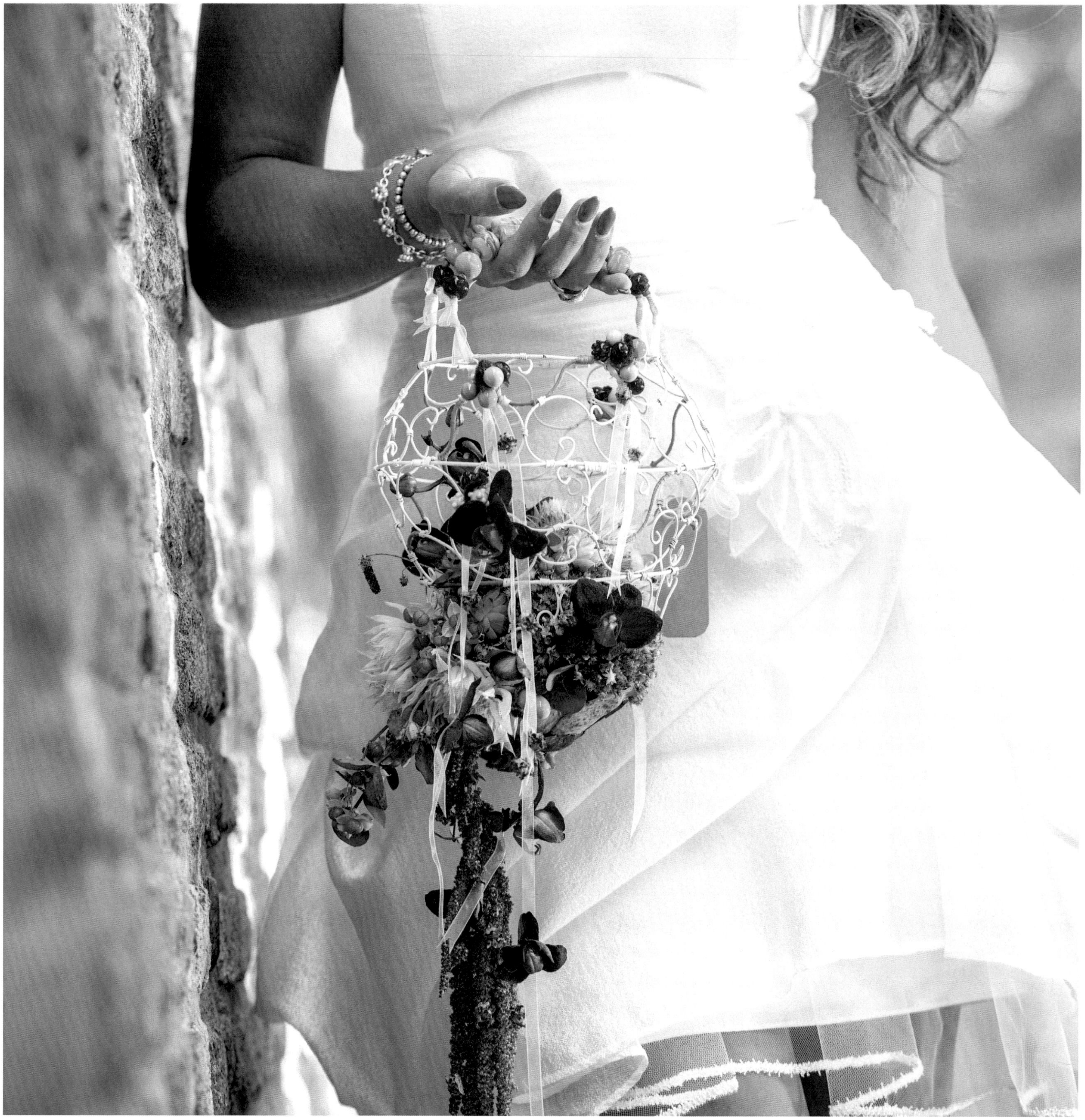

NADÈGE ROUX

Phalaeonopsis / Amaranthus caudatus / Ozothamnus rosmarinifolius / Celosia cristata red / Protea / Asclepias 'Beatrix, orange / Echeveria / Euonymius europaeus / Eucalyptus cinirea

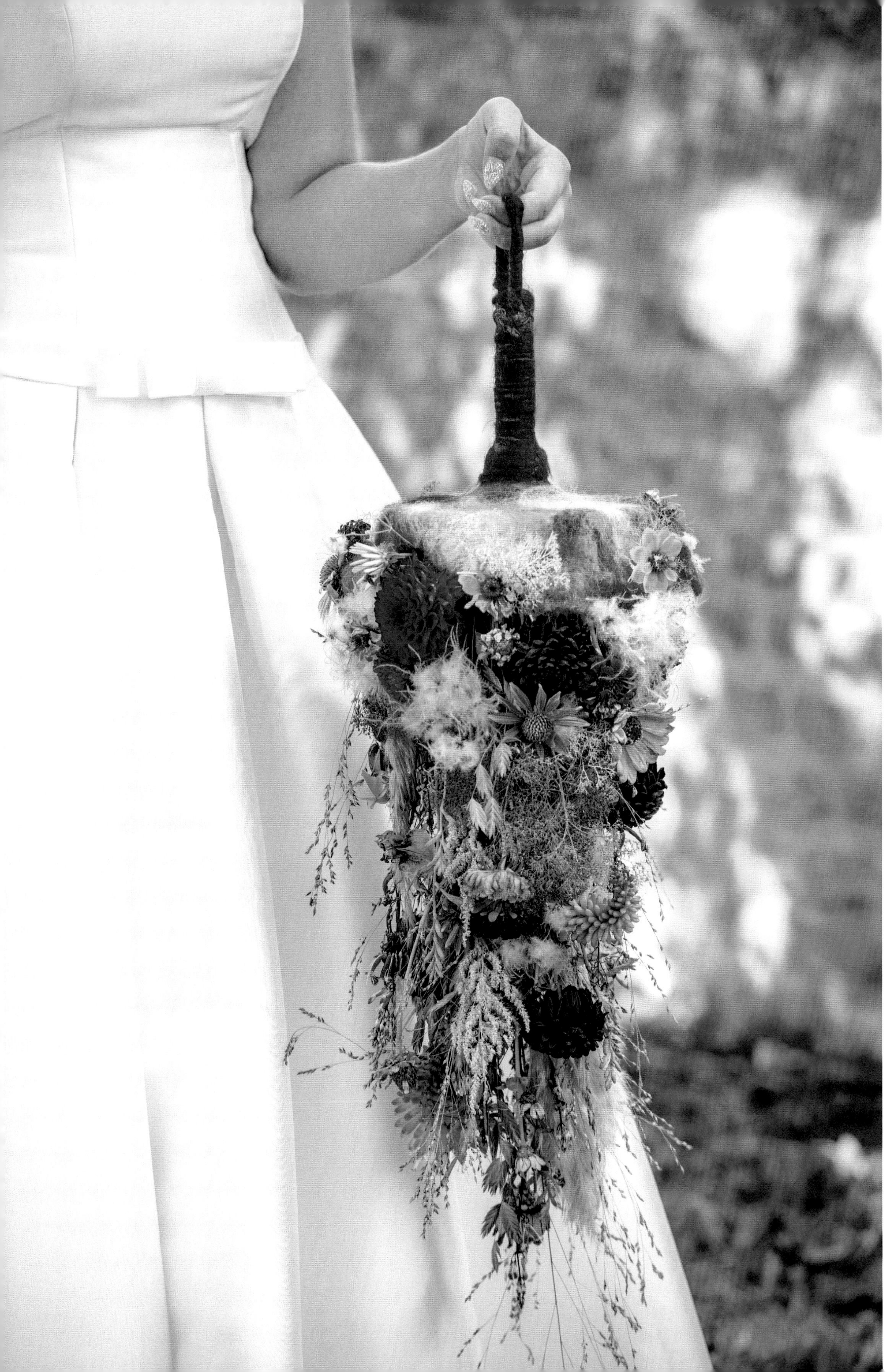

ADINDA SAP

Astilbe 'A Else Schluck'
Astilbe 'J. Europa'
Crocosmia 'George Davison'
Dahlia 'Ball Dark Spirit'
Kniphofia 'Alcazar'
Panicum 'Squaw'
Plectrantus 'Mona Lavende'
Zinnia
Echinacea
Clematis

“MADE WITH LOVE”

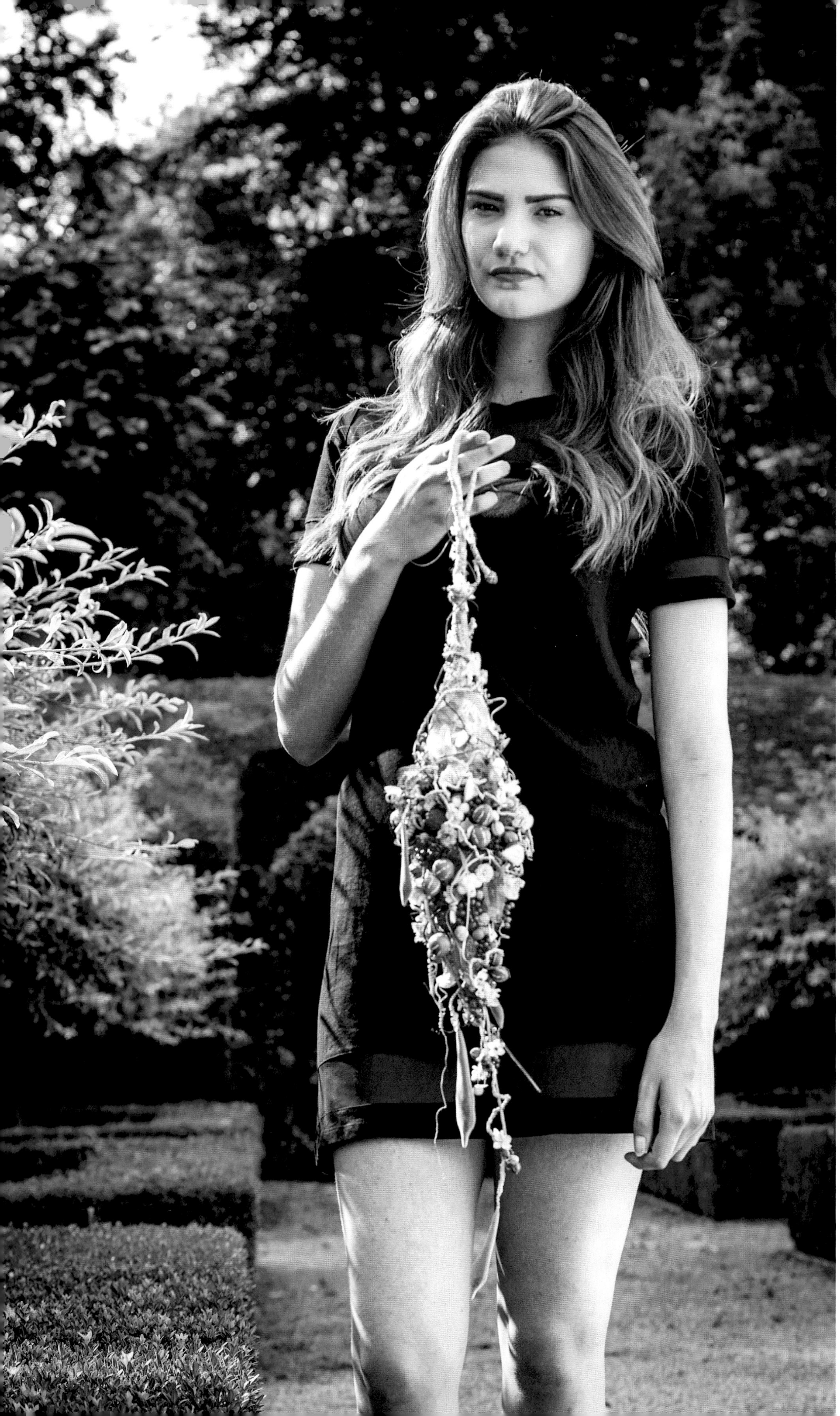

FRANK LEMMENS

Physalis
Phalaenopsis
Kalanchoe
Symphoricarpos
Ornithogalum
Schinus
Hydrangea
Diplocyclos
Cornus, fruit
Wisteria pods
Nigella

58

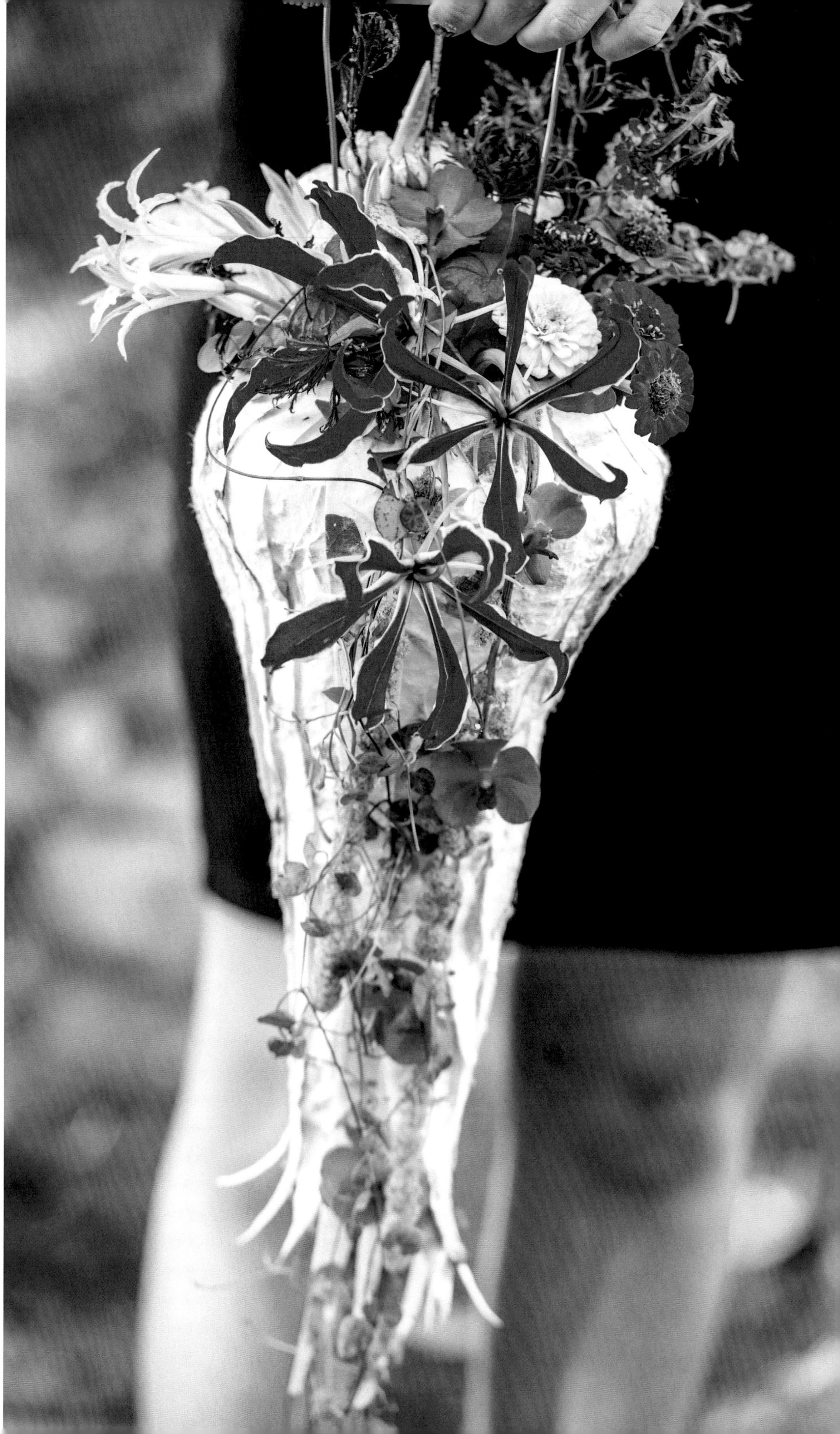

MIEKE HORSMANS

Acer palmatum dissectum
Nerine bowdenii
Gloriosa rothschildiana
Vanda
Amaranthus caudatus
Ceropegia woodii
Zinnia
Euphorbia fulgens

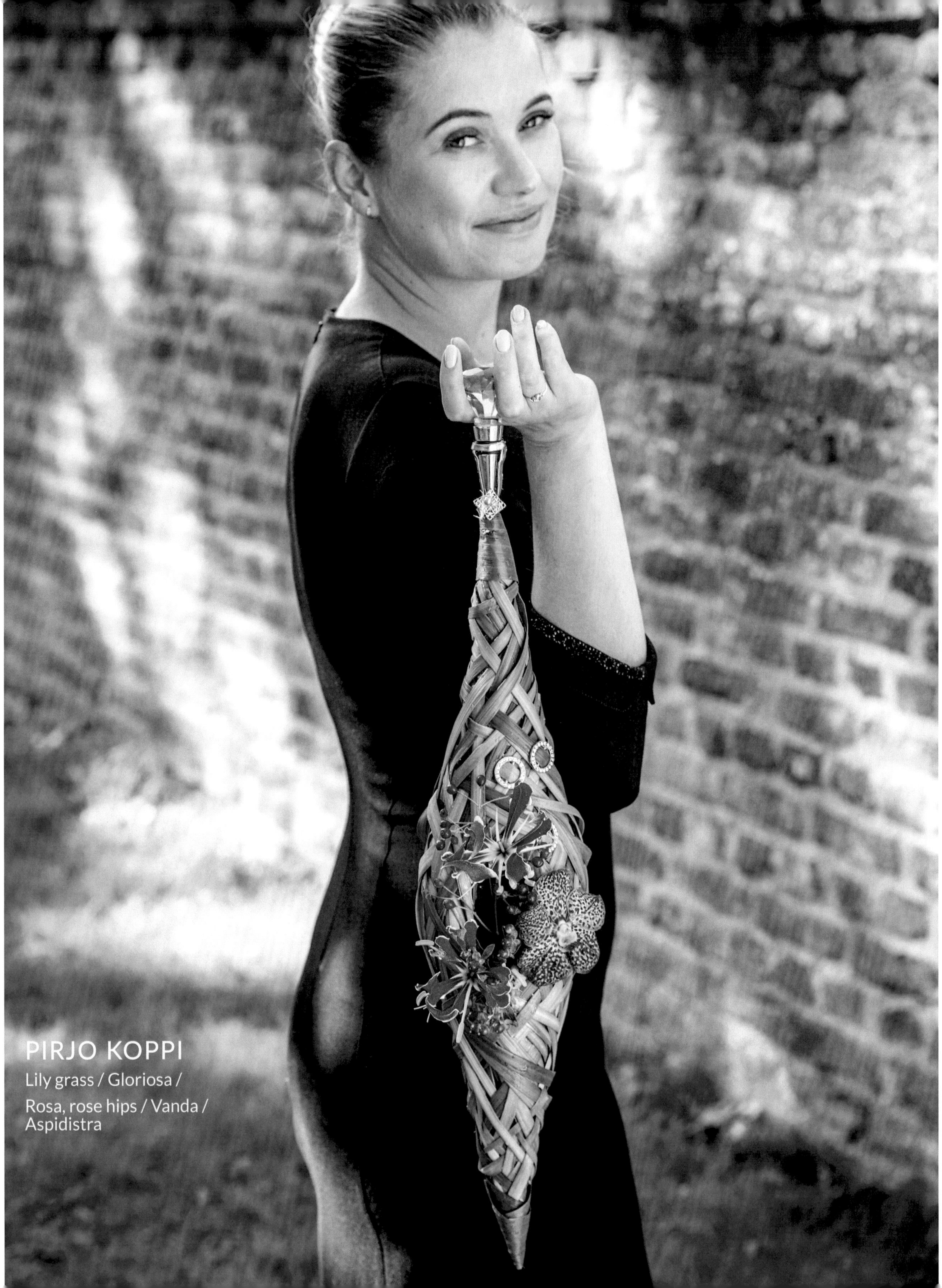

PIRJO KOPPI

Lily grass / Gloriosa /

Rosa, rose hips / Vanda /
Aspidistra

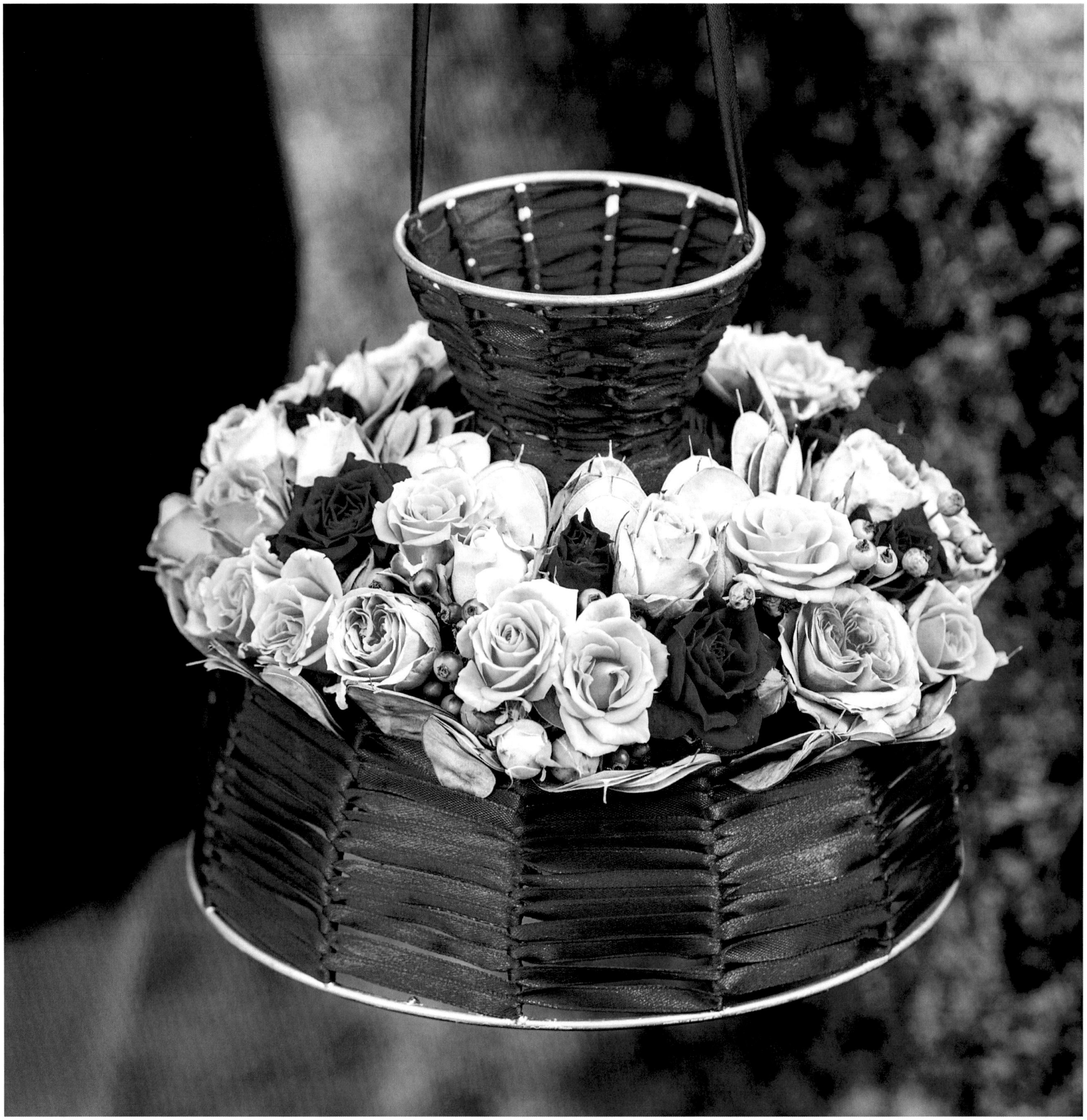

SARAH MEERSSCHAUT

Rosa 'Apricot', 'Mimi Eden' and 'Mirabel' / Lunnaria annua / Rosa, rose hips

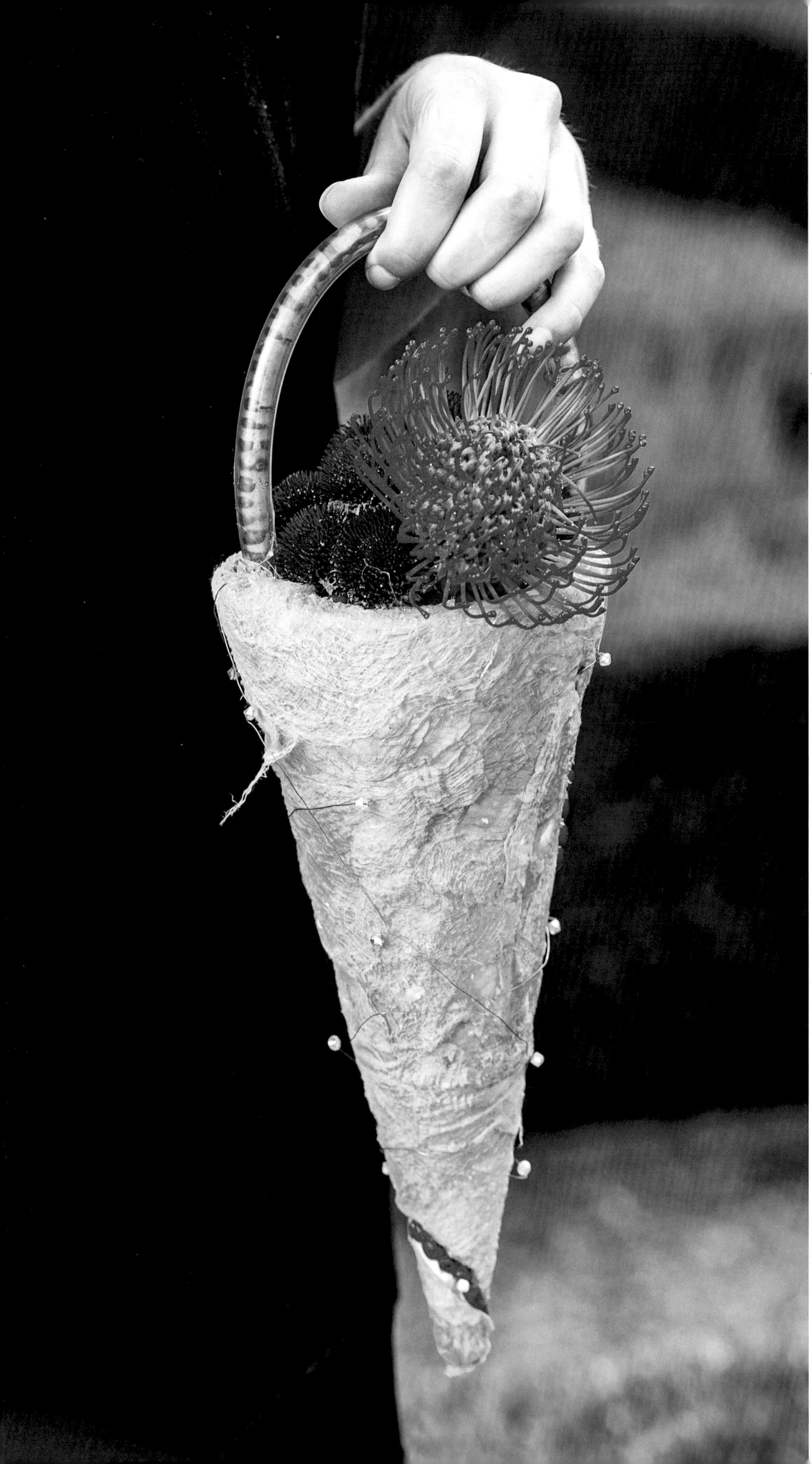

NATHALIE LAN DUNG

Rudbeckia nutans 'Emilia Red'

Morus

Sorbus aucuparia

Leucospermum

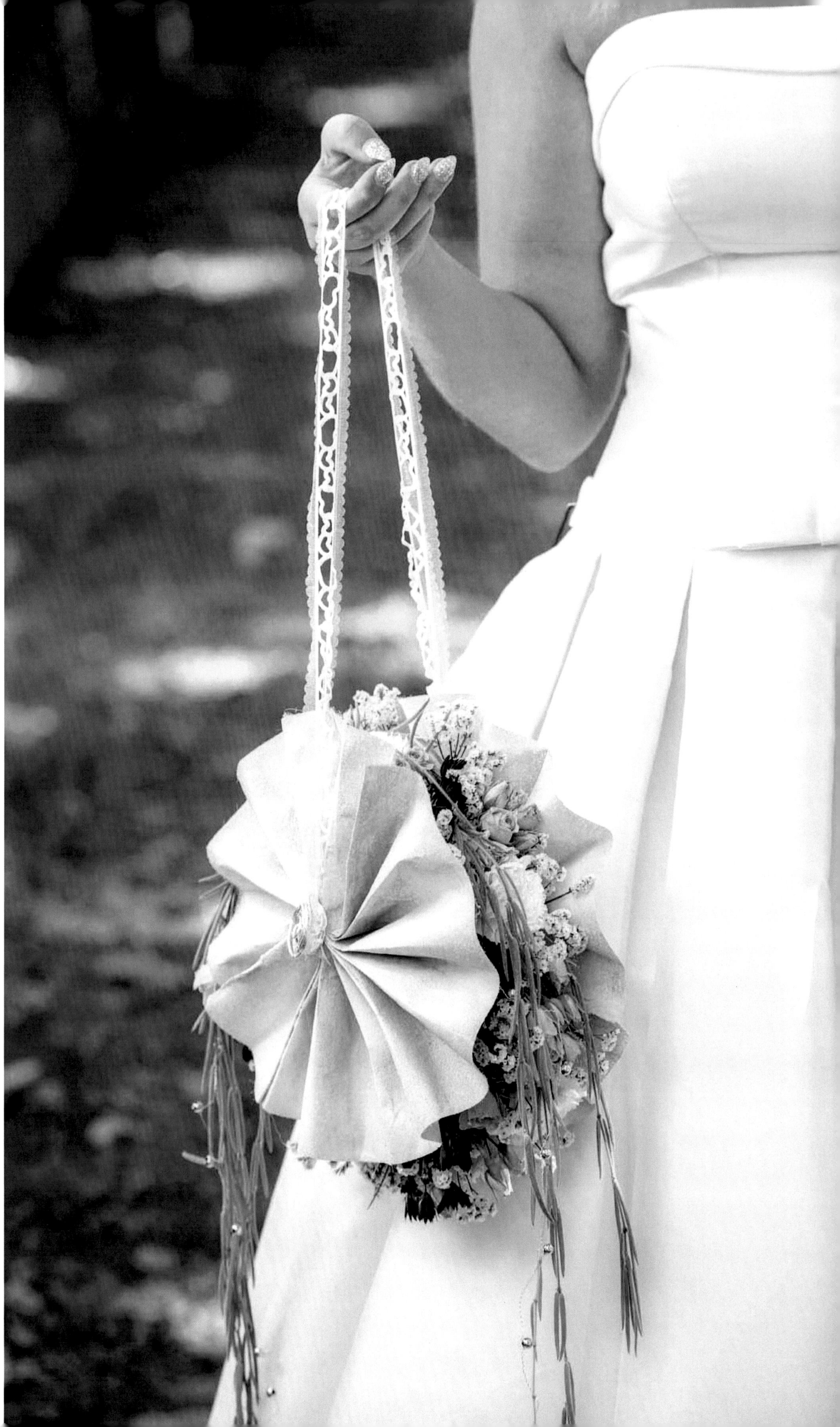

MARTINE DESSY

Dianthus 'Standard Delicia'
Hoya linearis
Rosa 'Lydia'
Limonium sinensis 'Mountain Diamond'
Astrantia 'Star of Fire'

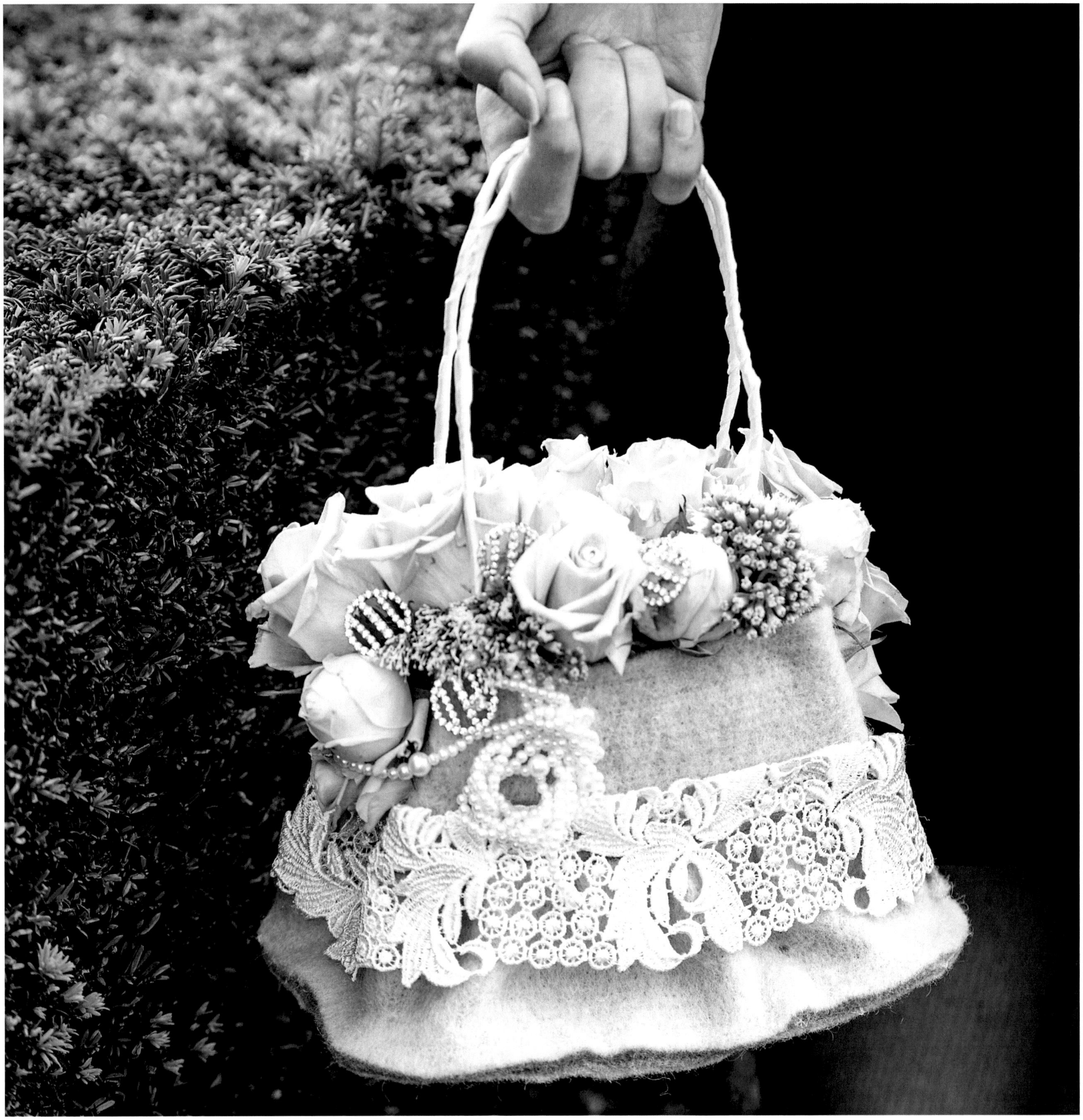

PASCALE PICHUEQUE

Rosa 'Menta' / Trachelium / Eupatorium / Rosa

ORIGINAL BOUQUETS

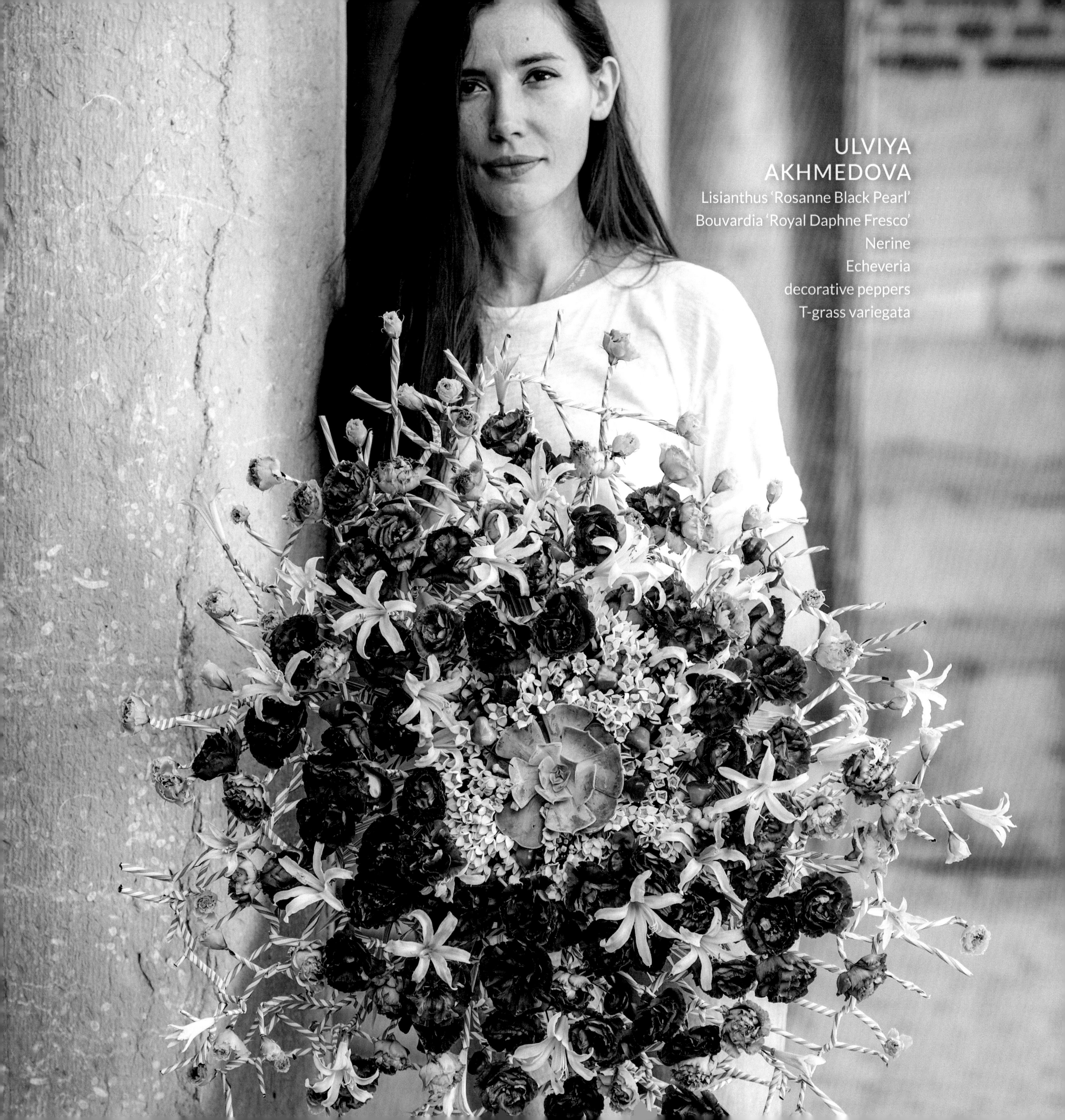

ULVIYA AKHMEDOVA

Lisianthus 'Rosanne Black Pearl'
Bouvardia 'Royal Daphne Fresco'
Nerine
Echeveria
decorative peppers
T-grass variegata

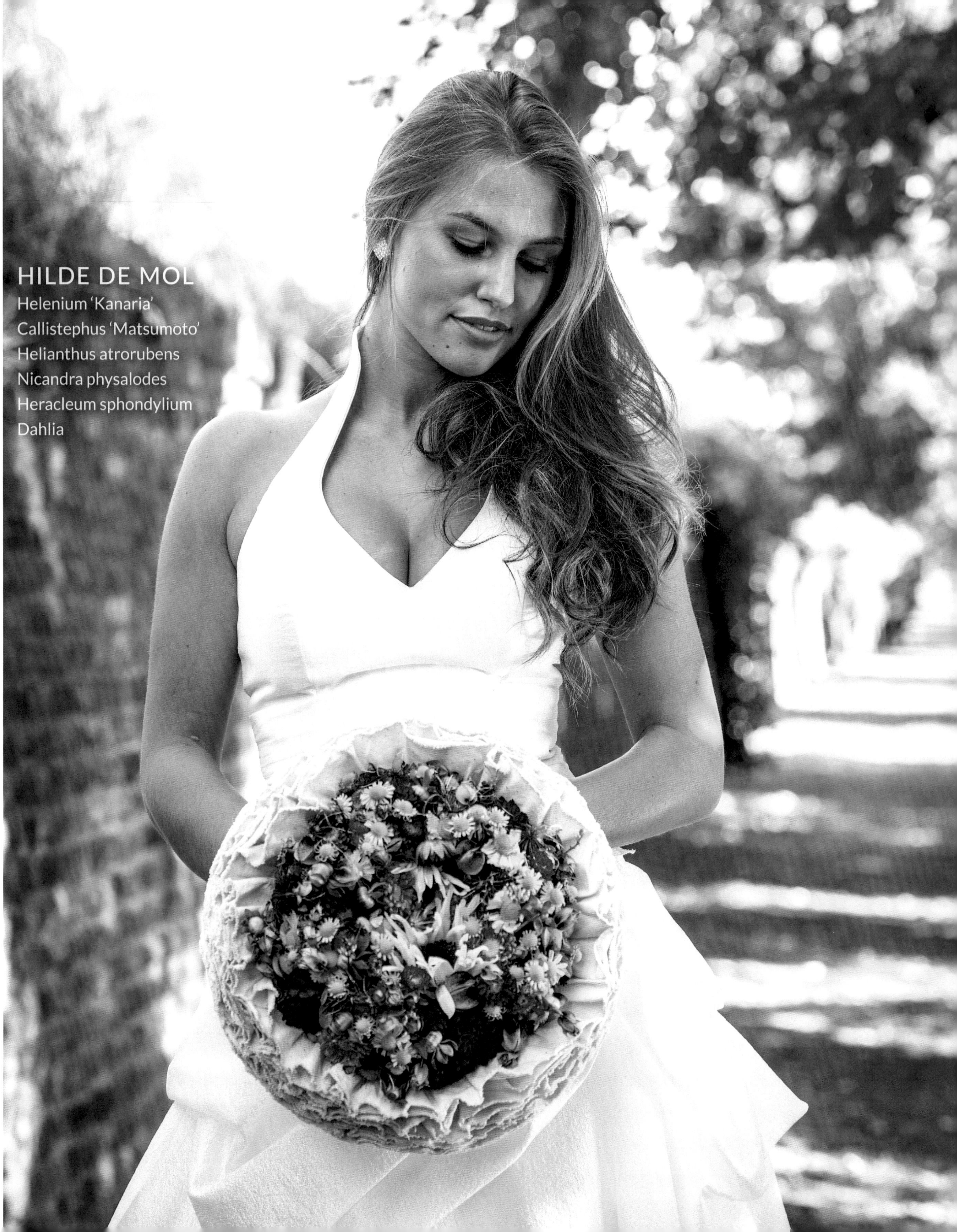

HILDE DE MOL
Helenium 'Kanaria'
Callistephus 'Matsumoto'
Helianthus atrorubens
Nicandra physalodes
Heracleum sphondylium
Dahlia

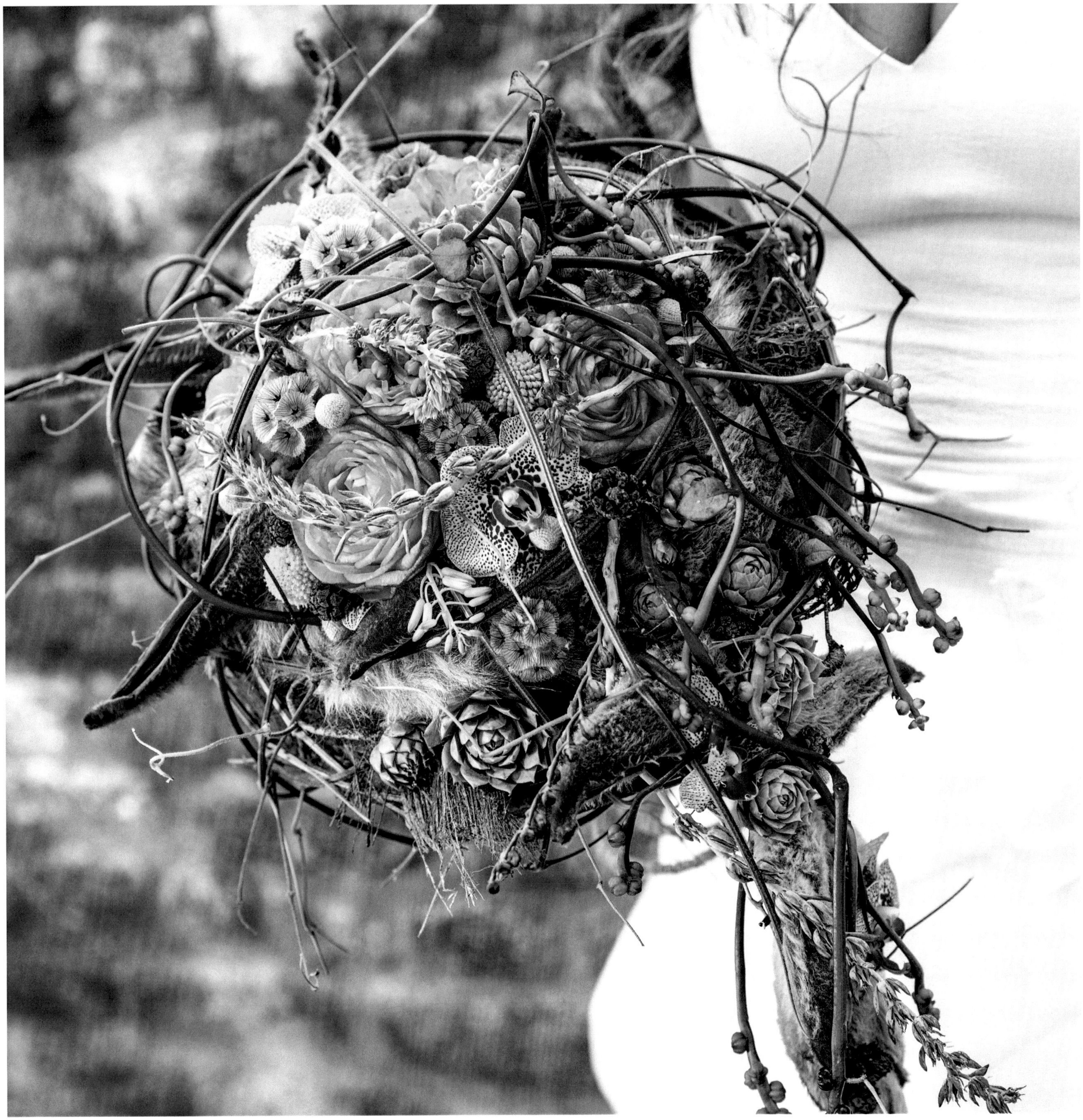

MIEKE HORSMANS

Heleconia / Phalaenopsis / Echeveria / Sempervivum / Scabiosa / Rosa Ecuador 'Free Spirit' / Bassella / Graspedia / Clematis / Cypress

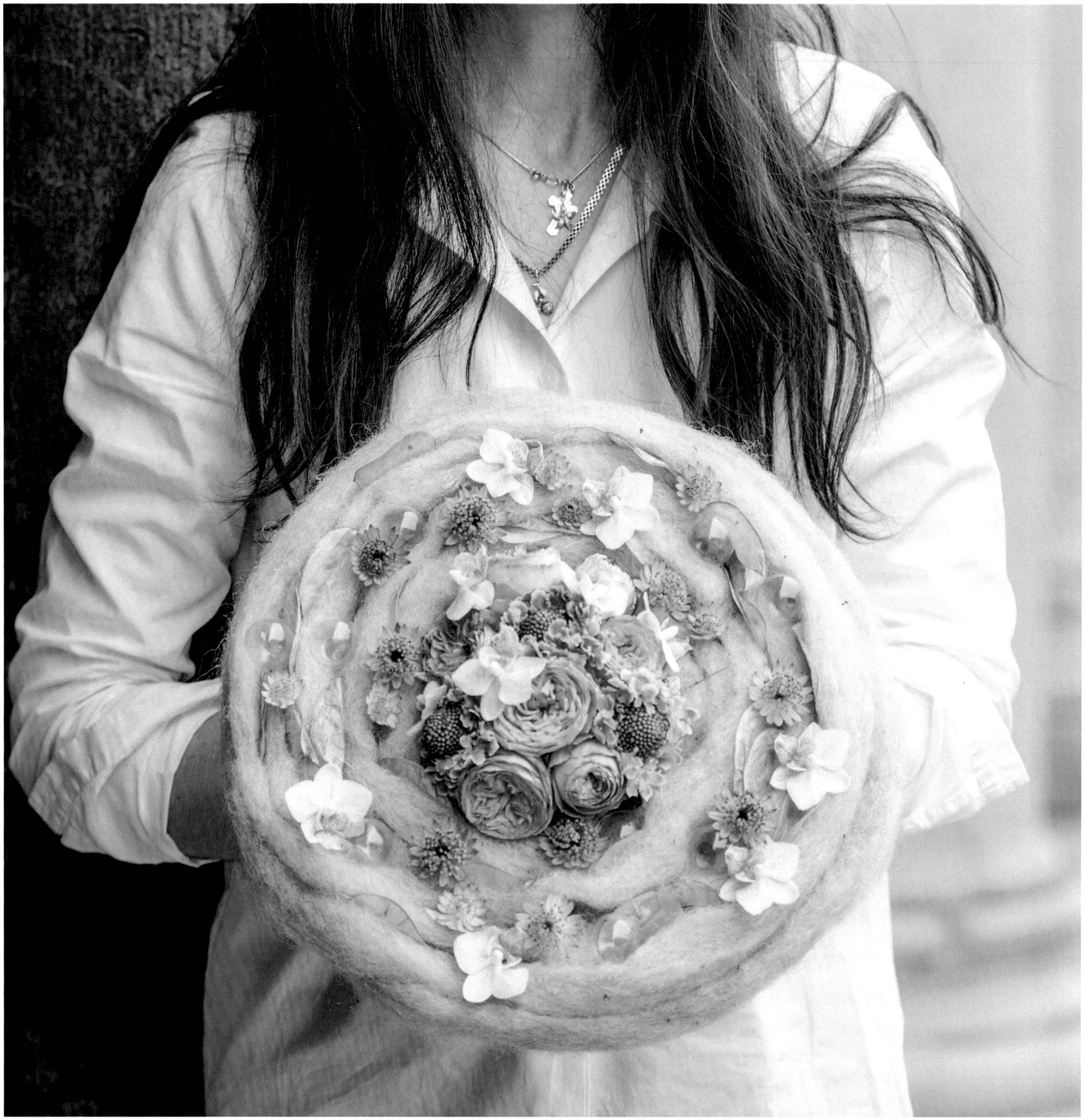

ULVIYA AKHMEDOVA

Lunaria / Scabiosa 'Marshmallow Scoop' / Rosa / Astrantia 'Star of Africa' / Phalaenopsis multiflora

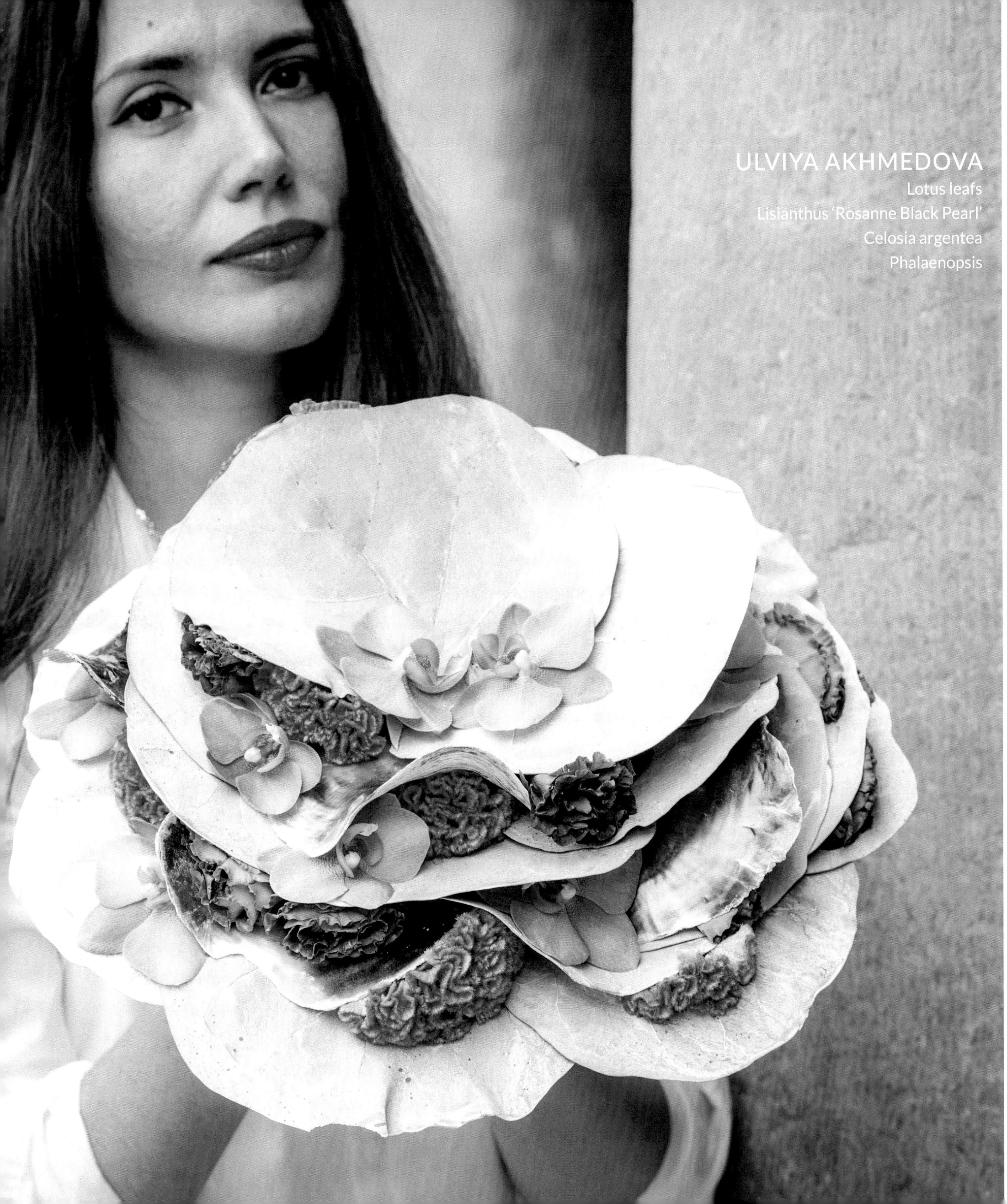

ULVIYA AKHMEDOVA

Lotus leafs
Lisianthus 'Rosanne Black Pearl'
Celosia argentea
Phalaenopsis

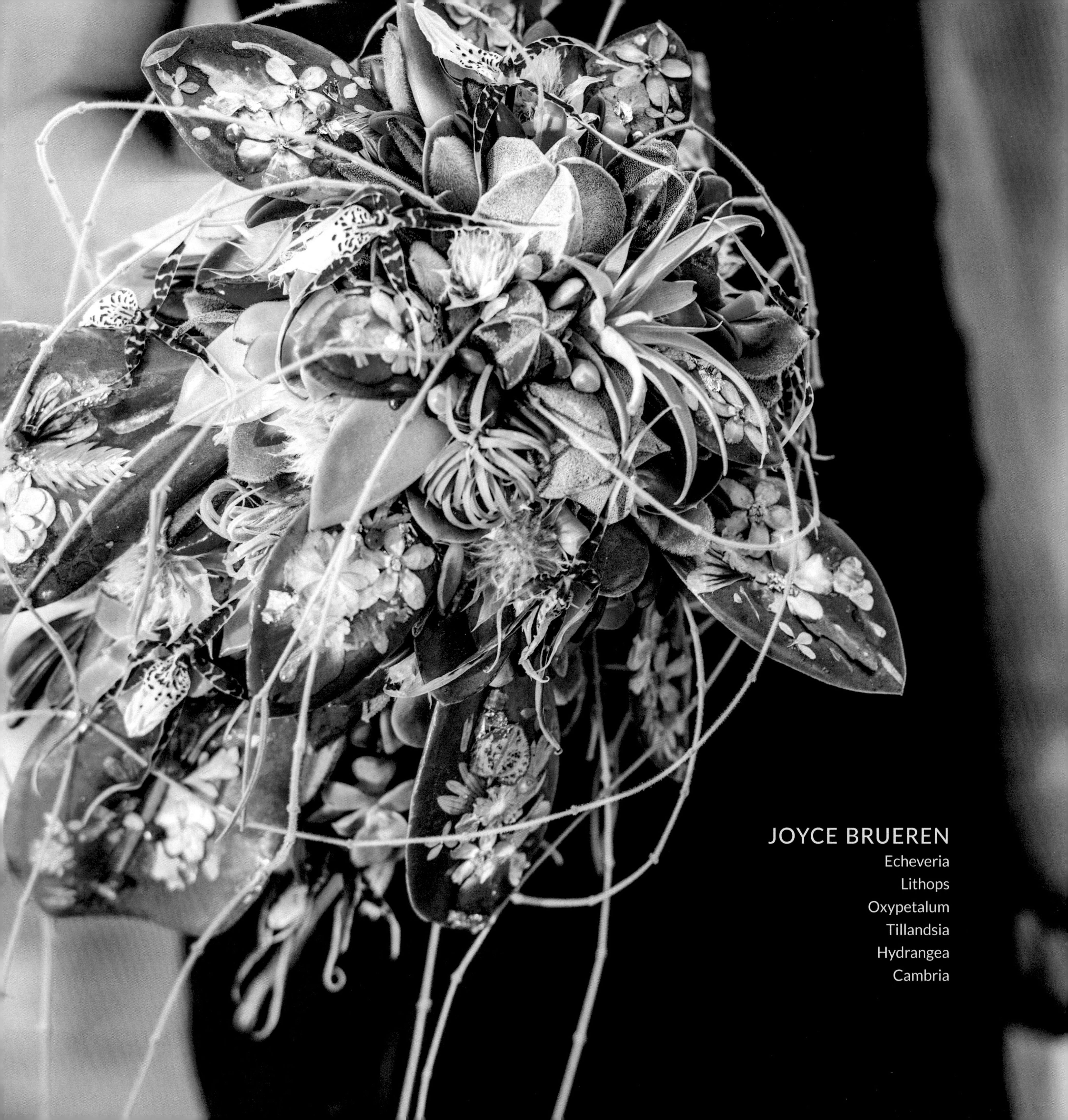

JOYCE BRUEREN
Echeveria
Lithops
Oxypetalum
Tillandsia
Hydrangea
Cambria

“

SOMETHING
OLD
SOMETHING
NEW
SOMETHING
BORROWED
SOMETHING
BLUE

”

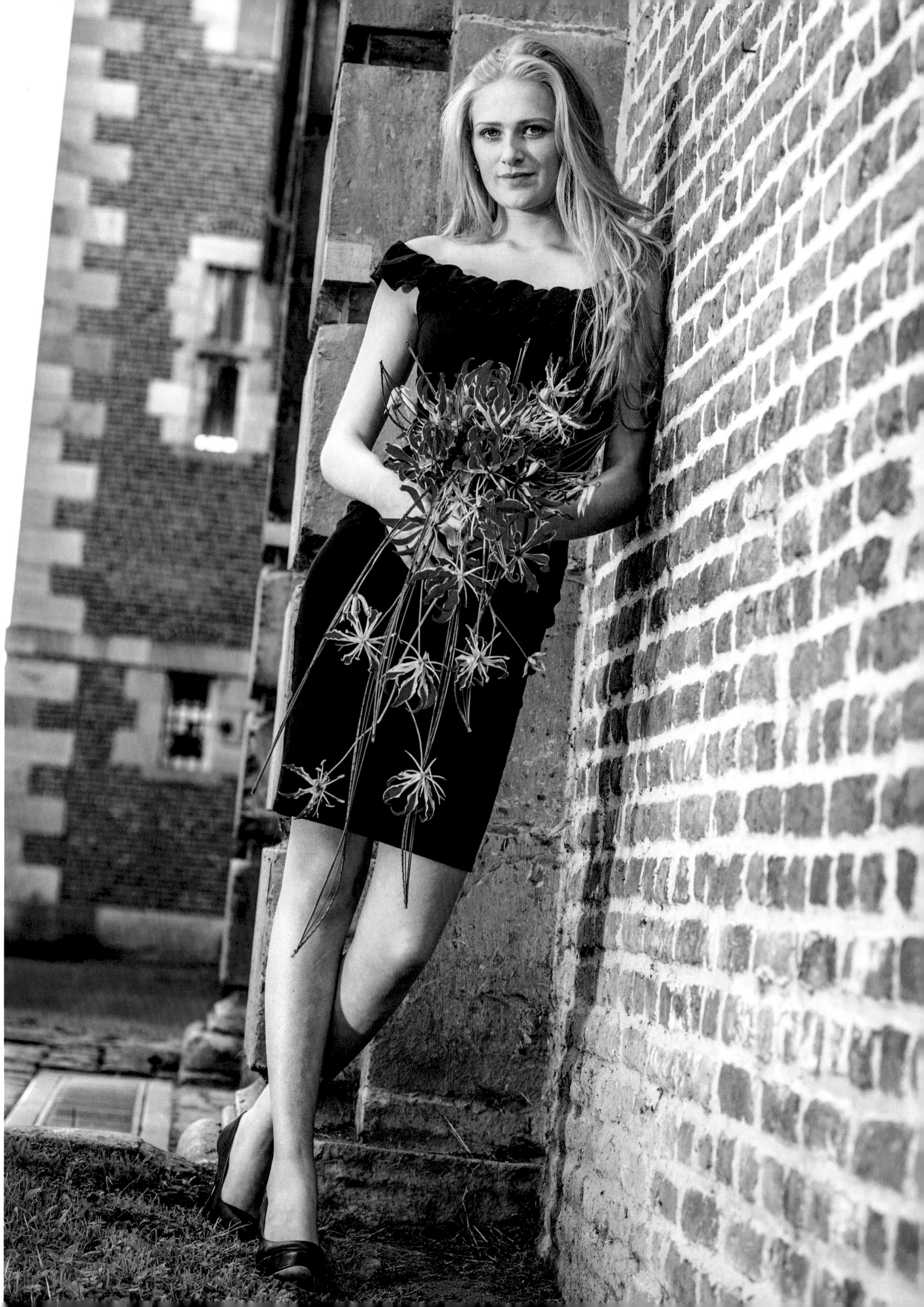

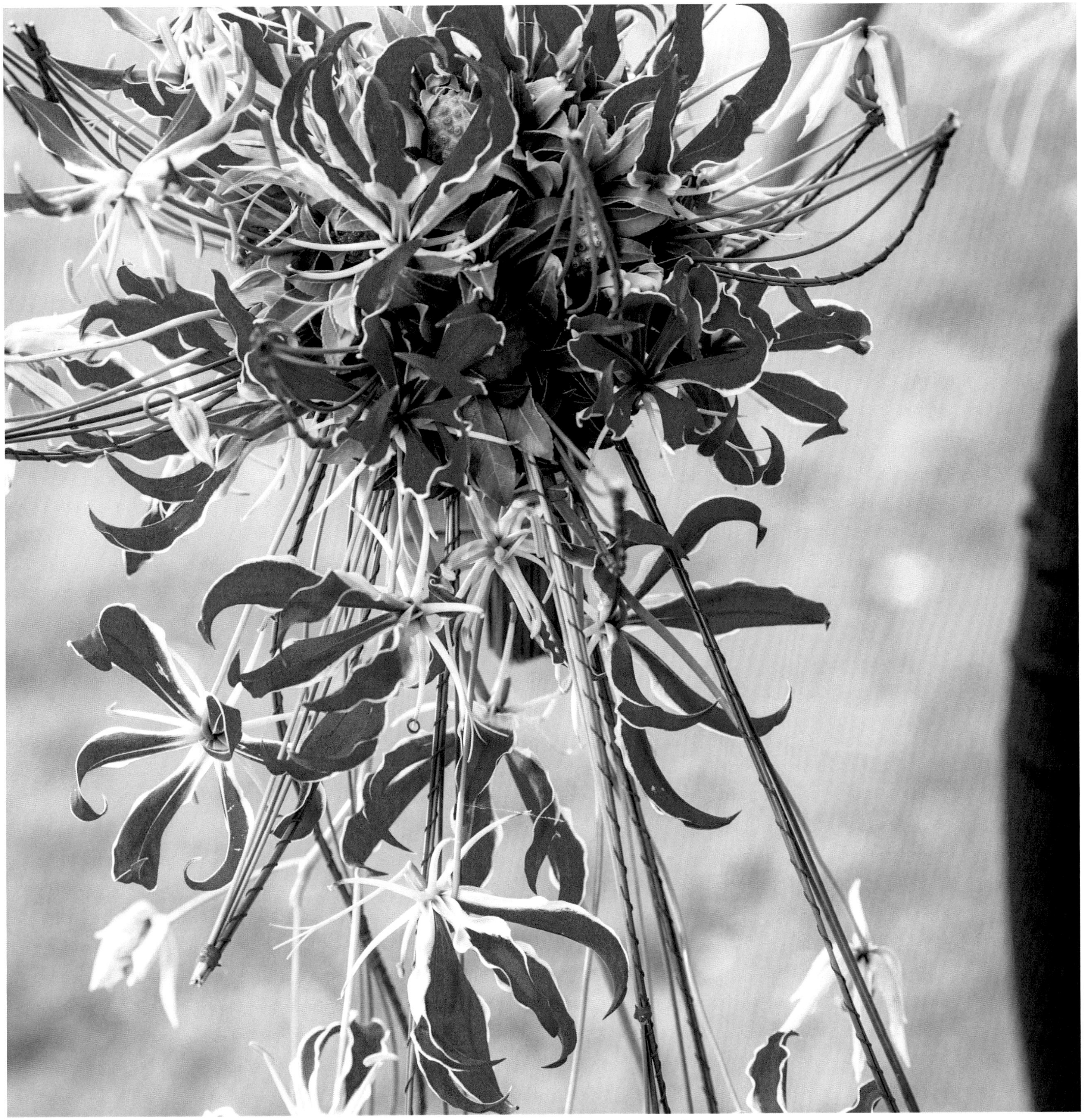

SONIA JONNIAUX

Gloriosa rothschildiana / Schoenus melanostachys (flexi grass) / Euonymus japonicus 'Microphyllus' / Cornus

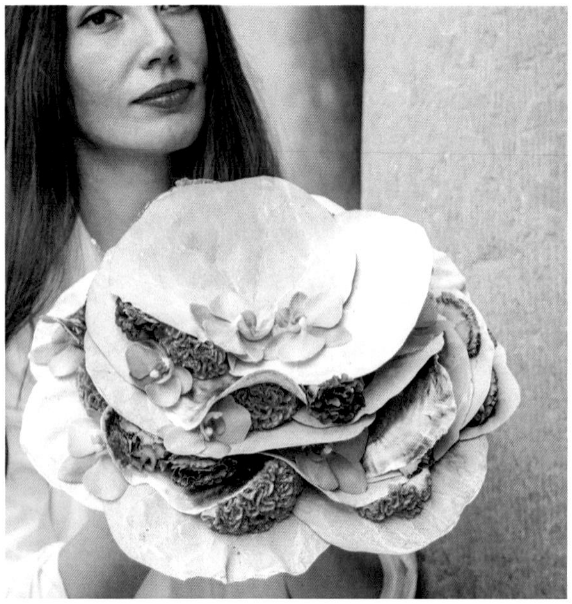
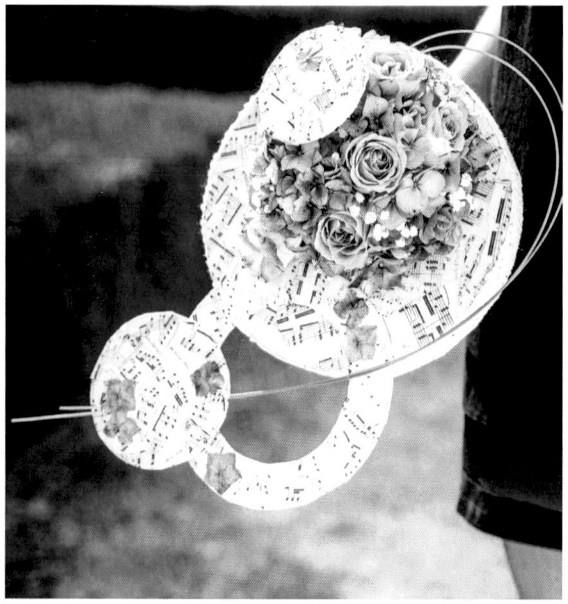
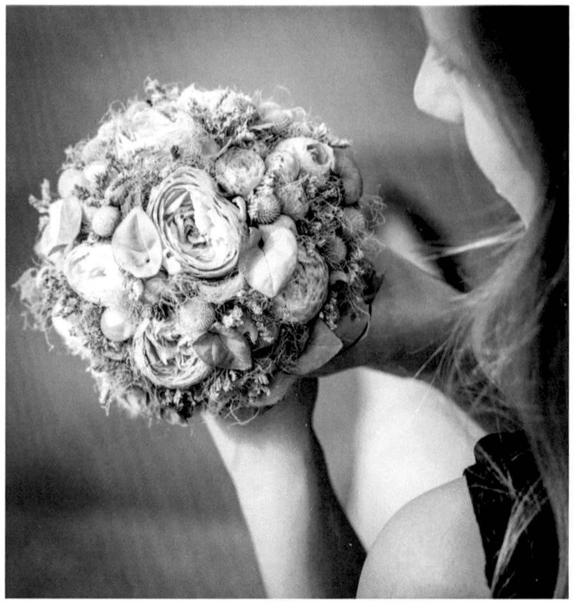
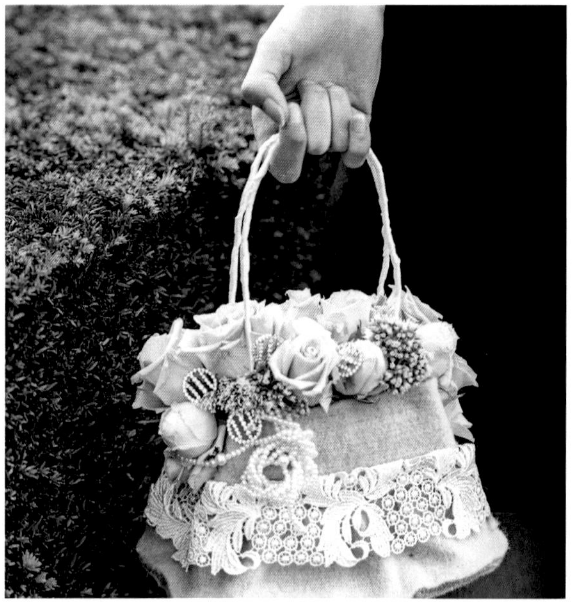
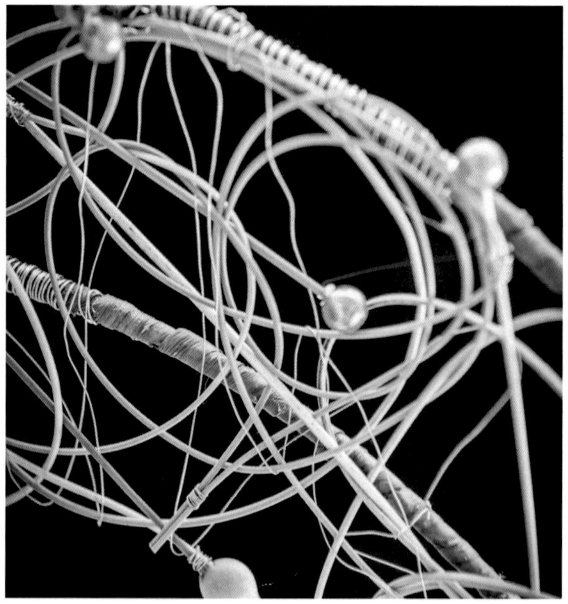
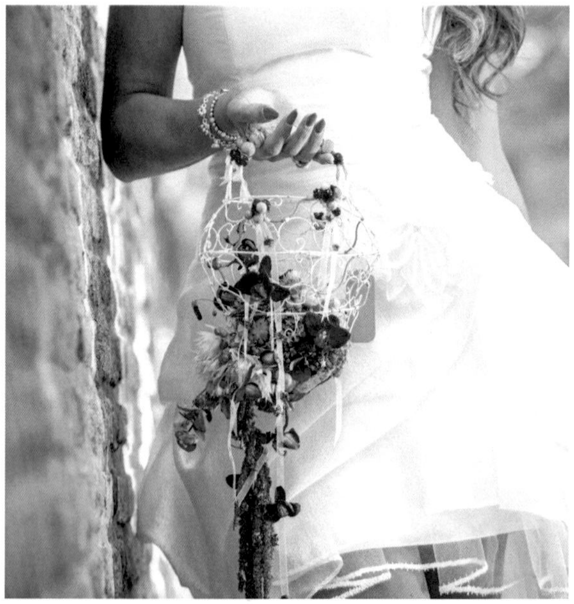
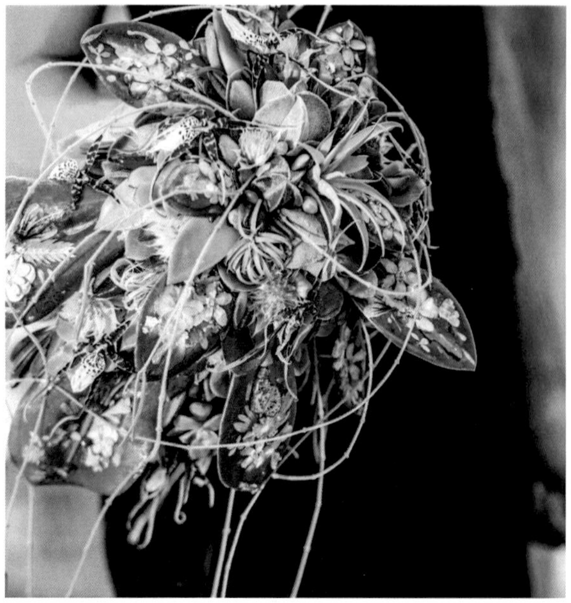
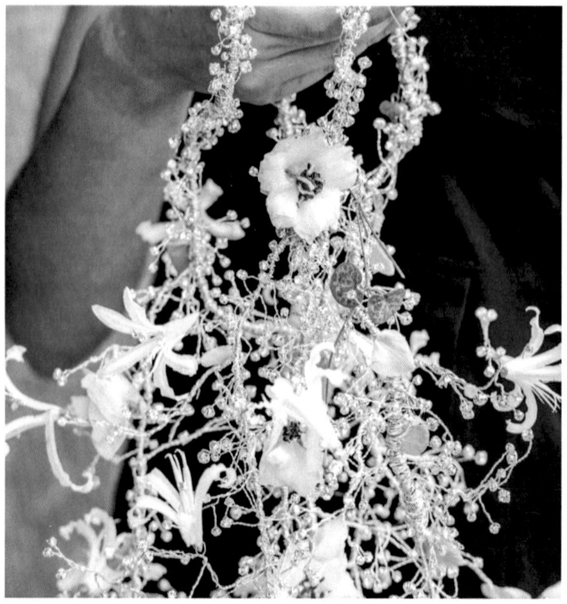
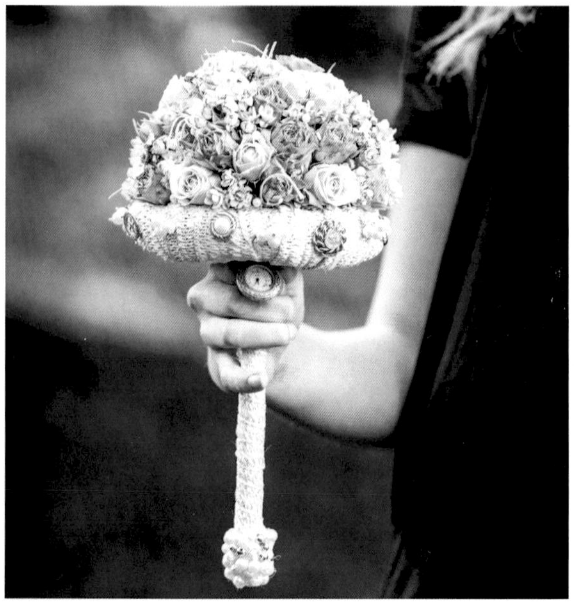